Cop's Kid

Cop's Kid

A Milwaukee Memoir

Mel C. Miskimen

THE UNIVERSITY OF WISCONSIN PRESS
TERRACE BOOKS

The University of Wisconsin Press
1930 Monroe Street
Madison, Wisconsin 53711

www.wisc.edu/wisconsinpress/

3 Henrietta Street
London WC2E 8LU, England

1   3   5   4   2

Printed in the United States of America

Library of Congress Cataloging-in-Publication Data
Miskimen, Mel C., 1955–
Cop's kid: a Milwaukee memoir / Mel C. Miskimen.
    p.   cm.
ISBN 0-299-18880-9 (cloth: alk. paper)
1. Miskimen, Mel C., 1955– —Childhood and youth.
2. Fathers and daughters—Wisconsin—Milwaukee.
3. Milwaukee (Wis.)—Biography.
    I. Title.
CT275.M555 A3   2003
977.5′95044′092—dc21   2003005022

Terrace Books, a division of the University of Wisconsin Press, takes
its name from the Memorial Union Terrace, located at
the University of Wisconsin–Madison. Since its inception in 1907,
the Wisconsin Union has provided a venue for students, faculty, staff,
and alumni to debate art, music, politics, and the issues of the day. It is a
place where theater, music, drama, dance, outdoor activities, and major
speakers are made available to the campus and the community.
To learn more about the Union, visit www.union.wisc.edu.

To my Creative Writing teacher,
Miss Mary Lou Jellen

Contents

Contents

Acknowledgments

My punctuation is atrocious
Fate
My dad

Special Thanks

Kim Parsons
Judy Bridges and the Redbird writers
Jonathan Overby
Mark, Caitlin, and Gus

Introduction

My father joined the Milwaukee police force in 1951 because it had built-in job security and the work would be different every day. Not like the job he had in the foundry, where he worked next to his father and his uncles until he broke out in boils and then got a job digging graves—a job that cleared up his skin condition and solidified his relationship with my mother: "Fresh flowers! Oh, you shouldn't have!"

By the time I was born in 1955, my father had worked the ambulance detail, vice, and narcotics, had walked a beat, had driven a squad, and had come *this close* to delivering a baby. He was a cop. We were a cop's family and I was a cop's kid.

I thought everyone's dad came home from work, took off his gun belt, slung it over the back of the kitchen chair, threw his handcuffs on the counter, sat down at the dinner table, and talked about how he had spent his day trying to get a fat woman unstuck from her bathtub or investigating a crime scene where someone had tried to cut off someone else's head with a very dull knife and would have succeeded if it wasn't for that darned ol' spinal column. "Pass the chicken, please!"

In 1996 I needed something to do other than my job and picking up after three other people who are perfectly capable of picking up after themselves but don't.

I enrolled in a writing workshop that was offered in my former high school (where I got a D in Comparative Lit, but an A in Creative Writing), and I learned the mantra, "Write what you know."

So I wrote essays about the perils of dating when my dad was the law and didn't have to rely on parental staples like "Because I said so" or "As long as you're living under my roof . . ." but won any argument by quoting pertinent state statutes. After collecting a few rave reviews from the writing group, I decided to go public.

I dabbled in standup comedy, using material based on my experiences growing up with a cop for a father, and people liked it. Too bad I didn't. Standup wasn't for me—the smoky bars, the late nights, a room full of kids who think Adam Sandler is God. It gave me the courage I needed to call Jonathan Overby, host of Wisconsin Public Radio's variety show, *Higher Ground*. I told him what I did, what my essays were about. He asked whether I had any radio experience. Well, I was on a couple of times as the thirty-fifth caller; I figured that qualified. He booked me, and I've been a returning regular guest for more than two years. Forget stand-up. I prefer sit-down comedy—public radio.

I'm still amazed when people come up to me after the show and wonder whether I made all this up. Didn't everyone's father run each boyfriend's name through the computer down at H.Q.? Yeah, well, they would have if they could. My daughter is seventeen; if only my father were still on The Job . . .

Cop's Kid

The Case of the Missing Maidenform

I grew up in a two-bedroom, one-bathroom ranch-style house in a subdivision that popped up in a field after World War II. Kids outnumbered adults ten to one.

I never understood why our house was referred to as a ranch. In my mind, "ranch" conjured up images of the Barkleys' spread on *The Big Valley* or the Ponderosa on *Bonanza,* with their sprawling verandas and views of rolling hills, pine trees, and maybe a ramblin' river. We had no porch, only a stoop. And, as far as vistas go, our ranch looked out across a weed-free lawn and a winding river of concrete into a mirror image of our house with slightly different trim. Yep, my parents left behind the porch, the alley, and the narrow backyard for a breakfast nook, a patio, and a detached garage.

You wouldn't think that a guy who packed heat and acted like John Wayne would be into gardening, but my dad was. Well, I wouldn't call it gardening; it was more like horticultural domination. Dad trimmed the unruly yews into submission. He clipped the pine trees (one on each side of the front walk, for symmetry) into perfect cone shapes. He made two planters out of red brick that he filled with battalions of red geraniums spaced exactly a trowel's width apart. Anytime there was any evidence of dandelions or crabgrass in our lawn, Dad would be out there after work in his uniform, eradicating.

During the summers, the kids ran from yard to yard, jumped fences, and rode bikes up and down the sidewalks and driveways. When it was lunchtime, the mothers fed peanut butter and jelly sandwiches and cherry Kool-Aid to crowds of hungry cowboys, baseball players, and princesses.

It was a neighborhood where most of the women stayed home—minded the babies (a new crop every spring), cleaned, cooked, hung the laundry out on lines strung from wash post to wash post, and sunned themselves on aluminum chaise lounges when the weather was hot. Except for my mother. She worked in an office.

It was supposed to be temporary, just until we could make ends meet. But, I don't know, maybe the ends kept getting farther and farther apart, or maybe we got used to the extras that her salary allowed—family vacations to Glacier Park and Mount Rushmore, instead of the usual rented cabin on a lake up north.

My sister and I were latchkey kids. We came home from school to an empty house. We were driven home from school by Muriel "Lead-foot" Dombrowski, the neighbor up the block who took corners on two wheels and didn't know the meaning of a gradual stop. My forehead and the back of her front seat had quite an intimate relationship.

On the days he worked, Dad would have the dinner already started so that when my mother came home, all she had to do was heat it up on the stove. He walked a beat near some of the better restaurants in Milwaukee, and when it was cold, he could count on a cup of coffee and a few tips from the chef. We started to eat things made with red wine and spices other than salt and pepper. My mother was an okay cook; she just had a limited repertoire that involved a lot of canned goods. (I remember seeing my first fresh pea. I couldn't believe anything so green could be edible.) Her forte was baking and Jell-O mold-making.

Pets came and went. We had dime-store turtles that didn't survive the wash-and-rinse cycle in the Maytag, parakeets that yearned for freedom—my mother saw to it that they got it—and a series of dogs, ones that my sister found, but we had to give them back to the families that claimed them. Another one crawled behind our kitchen stove and foamed at the mouth one day. She got it from Kevin Weynar, the weird kid next door.

Kevin was two years older than I was. He was a muscular kid with a cowlick on either side of his head that stood up like little horns. His eyebrows met across the bridge of his nose in a V-shape. His teeth were little

and pointed. The mothers in the neighborhood referred to him as a demon.

He went to our Catholic grade school for a while
and then got expelled—rumor had it that he had
jumped on top of the altar in the church and then gone
through the sacristy eating all the packages of unconsecrated hosts. By the time the story got to the second
floor, not only had he jumped on the altar, but he had
also danced naked. And he didn't eat the unconsecrated
hosts: he got into the consecrated ones, and, when he
ate them, he spat blood.

Kevin was never allowed to mix with the other kids.
Any conversation about him was punctuated with a
list of don'ts. Don't make eye contact. Don't let him
know you're home alone—tell him Dad is in the basement or taking a nap. Don't let him into the house for
any reason.

His teenage sister, Peggy, wore her hair in a gravity-
defying beehive. She and Kevin played "Blame It on
the Bossa Nova" on the record player in their garage
over and over for the entire summer. That was the same
summer Peggy had to go away for a while.

All our neighbors mowed their lawns on Saturday
mornings. Kevin's dad pushed his rusty lawn mower
with his one good hand. He never used his right one.
He kept it sheathed in a black leather glove. My mother
told me that there had been an accident in a factory and
that he had gotten it crushed in a machine. But it didn't
hang there all noodly like my father's cousin Richie's

arm did (he had had polio). Mr. Weynar's hand was frozen in a permanent curve, like a mannequin at Penney's.

Mrs. Weynar would sit in their car parked in the driveway and smoke cigarettes. She never drove it. Kevin drove it. Until my father stopped him. I remember my dad grabbing Kevin by the front of his T-shirt, almost pulling him out of the car, and then Mr. Weynar giving Dad trouble—until Dad whipped out his badge and that was the end of it.

Saturday was washday. My mother went into the basement, got the whites out of the washing machine, and hung them out on the lines in the backyard. First the towels, then the sheets and pillowcases, the socks, all the underpants, and, on the last line in the back, her three bras. All white Maidenform cotton. That was all she owned, plus the one she had on. But once, when she went to take the laundry off the line, there were only two. She couldn't figure it out. Oh well. Maybe it was all tangled in a towel in the bottom of the washer and she had just missed it.

Mrs. Kopecki, who lived in the house on the other side of Kevin's, was a full-figured, Playtex 18-Hour kind of woman. Over the summer months she had lost track of two long-line Cross-Your-Heart bras (the kind that were supposed to lift and separate) and one 18-Hour girdle.

Missing bras and girdles weren't the topics of conversation over coffee or on the sidewalk after summer suppers when the mothers came out and picked up the tipped bikes and scooters.

They talked about kids, husbands, and home improvements.

The Weynars' house was a work in progress. Theirs was the only pink house with aqua trim in the neighborhood. Mr. Weynar started painting it in 1960, his gloved hand encased in a plastic bag if it was raining, and it still wasn't done when they moved out in 1973, after the incident.

I didn't find out what had happened until after I was grown up and married. I was over at my parents' house for Sunday dinner. I sat in the same spot at the same kitchen table I always had, the spot that looked out on Kevin's former yard.

"Dad, whatever happened to Kevin Weynar? I remember a big commotion one night and then it seemed like the next day they were gone."

My mother got up from the table to get more wine. "Go ahead, tell her."

Dad took a sip and finished buttering his Parker House roll. "I went outside to see what the hell the dog was barking at. It was late. And when I walked around the side of the house, there was that nut Kevin."

"In our yard?" I asked.

"Yep, he was peeking in our bedroom window, watching your mother getting ready for bed."

"God! What a little creep—pass the salad dressing," I said.

"Wait. There's more." My mother motioned with her butter knife for my dad to give me all the details.

"He had on lipstick, Mrs. Kopecki's 18-Hour girdle, and your mother's Maidenform bra. His hands were down inside the front of his pants—well, you know what I mean."

"Wow."

Blame it on the bossa nova.

Sting Ray Sting

I got my first brand-new bike when I was eight. It was a royal blue twenty-six–inch J. C. Higgins with white fenders. I picked that color combo because it came the closest to the colors of my dad's squad car. I wasn't a streamer-bell-basket type of person. The only extra I invested in was a battery-operated horn that mounted on the handlebars—my siren.

I patrolled the neighborhood on that bike. I never left the house without my pocket-size note pad and pencil, the choker-chain dog collar that didn't fit our dog anymore (it made an excellent "come along"),* and the little rolling pin from the Kenner Easy Bake Oven (my nightstick). Strapped to my beaded souvenir belt

---

* A come along was a piece of equipment—sort of a type of handcuff. The cop would tighten and twist one end of it around a perpetrator's wrist (ouch!) to get him to "come along." It only worked if the perpetrator was sensitive to pain. Most of the time, my father got swung around and punched with the suspect's free hand. It was abandoned as a piece of department-issued equipment.

from the Wisconsin Dells was an empty holster for a twenty-two-caliber starting pistol that my father didn't use anymore.

It was hot that day. Muggy. It was about ten-thirty. Already my Peter Pan–collared blouse stuck to my back. School was out for the summer. I was out on routine patrol when I spotted Jean and Jan, the Wysocki twins. They didn't look like twins. Jean was the one with white-blond hair, a younger version of her mother. Jan had jet-black hair and looked like their dad. They were in tears. So were their two friends. I pulled over.

"We got everything all set up—the Dream House, Barbie in her picnic outfit, and Ken sitting in the Dream Car . . . and then they came riding through and wrecked everything!" Jean wiped her nose with one of Barbie's bedspreads.

Outfits, still on the plastic hangers, were strewn all over the Pepto Bismol pink bedroom suite. Barbie, un-accessorized, was stuck headfirst in the yew bushes.

"Uh huh. Did you get a good look at the person or persons who did this?" The twins pulled themselves together and started to comb through the grass, looking for lost high heels. "I know this is a difficult time. But I'd appreciate anything. Any description at all," I said, getting out my note pad.

"Sting Ray bikes," Jan said. "They rode Sting Ray bikes with banana seats."

When a boy got a grip on those high handlebars and felt that banana seat between his legs, he was wired for wheelies and wipeouts. Front lawns. Curbs. Loose gravel (the looser the better). Pets. Small children. They were nothing but obstacles to be jumped over, skidded around, or wheeled across.

I didn't have much to go on. Most boys between the ages of six and sixteen rode Sting Rays. "What about the bikes? Can you tell me what color they were?" For two kids who paid such close attention to accessorizing Barbie ("She wouldn't wear that straw hat with the green sunglasses and the yellow shoes!"), they should have noticed something.

"I think one of them had a baseball card clipped in the back wheel."

That was a start. "I'll keep in touch."

It was going to be a long, hot summer if this bicycle bullying continued. Words of advice from the well-known TV lawman Barney Fife filled my head. "Nip it! Nip it in the bud! Nip it. Nip it. Nip it." But how? The Sting Ray rider could easily outmaneuver my clunky but serviceable J. C. Higgins. Road block? Nope. Speed trap? Hmmmmm.

The Wysocki twins agreed to be the bait. They pulled out all the stops. Two Dream Houses. The Dream Car. Ken, Midge, Skipper, Bubble-haired Barbie, and three pony-tailed Barbies—two blondes and one brunette. (Their mother worked part-time at Drew's Variety Store and got a discount on all things Barbie.) I used my mother's black hair dryer with the cord wrapped tightly around the handle as a speed gun and took my position between the maple tree and the mailbox.

They came around the corner.

They used the O'Rileys' hill to get airborne. "Ppppthppppthpppth." Their baseball cards fwapped against the spokes of their back wheels. Jimmy Mowpa and Danny Checusz. I should have known. They were a year younger than I was. They lived up the block. Next door to each other.

I clocked them going fast and on high heat.

They skidded into the first Dream House. The Wysocki twins held their ground. I bounded out from my hiding place. "All right, you two, that's enough!" I said, my legs wide apart and my hands on my hips.

"What the . . . ?" Danny said as he rested his elbow on his crossbar stick shift. Jimmy skidded to a stop, doing a neat fishtail with his back wheel.

"Whadya think you're doing? Racing through here like a bunch of demons?"

"What are you gonna do about it?" Jimmy said.

"No, James Mowpa and Daniel Checusz. The question is . . . what are YOU gonna do about it?" I bent down and confiscated the baseball cards from their back wheels—Jerry Kendall, Cleveland Indians, batting average .213, and Dal Maxvill.

"Ooooooooh, like I care about Jerry Kendall. Why do you think he's in my back wheel?"

"Yeah, I've got three more Dal Maxvill's in my drawer," Jimmy smirked.

"Evidence."

"Evidence of what? A bad batting average?"

"I'm taking these to your mothers. Wait 'til they

find out about your little escapade." Mrs. Mowpa and Mrs. Checusz were not the June Cleavers or the Aunt Beas of the neighborhood. They were the unanimated versions of Cruella DeVil or some Wicked Queen. They slapped first and asked questions later.

"Whoa. Whoa. Whoa. Wait a minute." Danny said. I knew that if I played the mother card, they'd see things my way.

"Suppose we settle this thing here and leave our mothers out of it?" Jimmy said.

"What have you got in mind?"

Danny pulled a melted Hershey bar from his back pocket. "How about this? You know . . . to forget the whole thing?"

"How about you keep away from the Wysocki twins?"

They consulted each other.

"Deal. And it's not because we're scared or anything . . ."

I looked at the Wysocki twins. "Deal," said the twins. "Only you've got to help us find the other red high heel."

I left them combing the grass. Jimmy asking Jean whether the Dream Car could do wheelies. Danny wanting to put Skipper in her Girl Scout outfit. Case closed. The streets were safe. Harmony restored. I got on my bike and went home to type up my report.

Barbie Crime Scene

On really hot summer days, when it was too hot to ride bikes down to the public pool and even going out on routine patrol was too much of an effort, I'd drag the card table out to the garage, throw down some old blankets on the cool, grease-stained concrete floor and invite the twins Jean and Jan Wysocki over for an afternoon of Barbies.

It was an effort to coordinate the transportation via wagons and bicycle baskets: Dream Houses, Dream Cars, Kens, Alan (there was only one), Skippers, Scooters, Midges, all the different versions of Barbie (bubble-haired, dark-haired pony-tailed, blonde pony-tailed), and several carrying cases full of outfits for every possible occasion. And then it took forever to set up—dreaming up the perfect scenario, deciding on outfits.

"I want Ken to be coming to pick Barbie up for a picnic that they're going to have over there, next to the grass cutter. See, Ken just got home from college and he hasn't seen Barbie in months and then he calls her and they go out for a picnic!" That was Jean's favorite scenario. The Picnic. Or the Sleigh Ride. Ken was always coming home from college. Hadn't seen Barbie in months. Calls her on the phone. Blah, blah, blah.

"No. Midge is Barbie's maid, and she is really in love with Ken, but Barbie won't let her see him because . . . she's . . . really a wicked queen." Jan had this thing about wicked queens. Evil kings. She had an extra Ken that their dog had got hold of one day. There were big gouges in his left arm and leg and in his face. He was perfect for Evil/Wicked King/Prince Ken. But we had played that so many times. Dog-Eaten Deformed Ken locks Barbie away; Well-Dressed Ken comes to the rescue and stiff-arms Half-Eaten Ken, causing him to fall to his death from the top of our doghouse; Ken and Barbie kiss (in that awkward way since they lacked bendable arms); and then we spend the rest of the afternoon planning the wedding.

"Hey, I've got an idea," I said. "How about—there's been a murder in one of the Dream Houses!"

"A murder?"

"Okay. Let's say Barbie is having a party at her Beach House and the neighbors call the police because the party is really loud."

"I don't think Barbie would be having a loud party. She's not supposed to be wild." Jan wasn't buying it.

"Yeah, well she's not supposed to be a wicked queen either!"

"Then what happens?" I could always count on Jean to see my side of things.

"Okay, so in the meantime, Ken falls from the second-story balcony and lands in the pool. His body is discovered by Skipper and Scooter, who have been at the party spying on Barbie."

"Why?" asked Jan.

"Why what?"

"Why are they spying on her?"

"Because they're never invited to anything that might be fun. You know, they're like the obnoxious little sisters that are always hanging around."

"Wait a minute. Why did Ken fall from the balcony?" asked Jean.

"Because he and Barbie were having a fight over her relationship with Alan."

"I know. Ken is mad because Alan has gone out with Barbie while he was away at college." I figured she'd work the "away at college" theme in there somewhere.

"So, she pushed him?" asked Jan.

"Not necessarily."

They liked it. We spent the next hour or so getting all the dolls into their swimsuits, typecasting Dog-Eaten Ken as the victim, positioning them, putting together a police outfit for one of the Kens using bits and pieces from his yachting ensemble and his snappy business suits.

"So who ends up finding Face-Down-in-the-Swimming-Pool Ken?"

"Skipper, because she saw the whole thing."

"And then what?" asked Jean.

"Well, after Police Officer Ken gets a statement from Eyewitness Skipper, Two-Timing Barbie starts up the Dream Car and backs over her."

"So now she's killed Ken *and* Skipper?" asked Jan, putting the finishing accessory, a gold pin, on Police Officer Ken's uniform.

"Midge can be the neighbor who calls," said Jean, positioning her with the pink princess phone in her hand. Midge was always the character actress in our plays. She was the maid. The cleaning lady. The neighbor.

It went well. Better than I had expected. Every time we played Barbies and settled on who was going to do what to whom, there was always that unexpected great moment that no one scripted. After Jean backed the Dream Car over Skipper (two times to be sure the job had been done), she drove it full speed into the table leg. Barbie's head hit the windshield; the driver's side door opened, and she flew out.

I got my sidewalk chalk and drew an outline around her hideously bent body. Jan covered her up with a pink bedspread. And Forensic-Evidence-Gathering Barbie did her job dressed in a fabulous tweed suit and matching pillbox hat, accessorized with white gloves, a note pad and a camera.

In the Matter Of:
The Beatles

Having a cop for a father worked to my advantage, sometimes. During big events, if Dad was working, he finagled us seats up front, or he got us in the "back" way. Events like the Circus Parade, or maybe the Ice Capades. Events that weren't that important. So when I heard the big news that the Beatles were coming to Milwaukee, I assumed Dad would be able to get my sister, our friends, and me in. Or at least get us some tickets.

Never assume.

I don't remember how Beatlemania invaded our house. Probably, like a cold, my older sister brought it home. She was four years older than I, and worldlier in matters of all things hip. She kept track of the top ten records played on local radio, had endless debates with her girlfriends as to which radio station was better, WOKY or WRIT, and had stacks of *16* magazine, with covers screaming, "Win a Dream Date with Paul!" or

"John! Two Full-Color Photos of Your Fave Beatle!!!" or "The Dave Clark Five vs. the Beatles! Cast Your Vote Inside!!"

I wasn't interested in dating any Beatle—more than anything, I wanted to be a Beatle. The four of us set up in Ann Mrocynski's garage (the only one with an electrical outlet to plug in the record player). Ann was Paul. Diane was Ringo. Jean was George. I was John. We made guitars out of cardboard and glitter. We had a coffee can and bucket drum set, broom handles in flowerpots for mikes. We lip-synched to the latest 45s (both A and B sides) until we had it right. Ann made us practice from right after school until it got dark or until her dad came home from work and wanted to park the station wagon in the garage, whichever came first. On the days when the garage was in use, we'd work on our Liverpudlian accents: getting the right tone, using words like "gear," "fab," and "loo" as if we'd been using them forever.

We had to be content with seeing the Beatles in magazines or on album covers. Occasionally there'd be a report from London on the *CBS Evening News,* the four of them in their slim-fitting suits getting pushed into a black car and whisked away amid swarms of girls wearing big boxy coats and black flats. My father watched with amusement as his British counterparts, the bobbies, stood with their arms linked, grimacing, while heaving waves of screaming girls tried to break through. He knew what that was like. He'd worked enough crowd control in his fifteen-year tenure on the force. Enough to hate crowds. That's why we never went anywhere, except camping.

My dad raised us to think for ourselves. To use logic. To solve problems by using what was available. He took my sister and me fishing, hunting, hiking. He made us bait our own hooks, clean our own catches. We learned to play with the little hurts. Cramps? Walk 'em off!

He often referred to me as the son he never had. In the grocery store, he refused help from the teenage boy bagger. "No, thanks. My boy will get it," he'd say, nodding his head toward me. I was skinny and flat-chested. Tall for my age. Gangly. Not a real "looker." I wore jeans and T-shirts that my father bought me at the army surplus store. He was convinced that my sister and I would be above all this girlish swooning. No daughters of his would be caught crying over some guys from England with funny haircuts. Nope.

I sat cross-legged in front of our RCA television set, straining to hear over the din of a typical Sunday evening at our house. My dad, uncles, and grandfather had a raucous pinochle game going. My mother and my aunts were busy replenishing chip and dip bowls, washing the dishes, gossiping. My cousins were fighting over prime real estate on the sofa. My sister made sure that she had the television set turned on ten minutes before the *Ed Sullivan Show* came on, to warm up the tubes.

"Ladies and gentlemen, *the Beatles!*"

There they were. In my living room. In glorious black and white. Each one getting his own close-up. A trickle of sweat traveled from John's sideburn down to his recently shaved jaw. Paul's eyelashes had never looked so long. George was angularly handsome. Ringo? Well, from the right angle . . .

All the commotion on the TV—the sobbing, the hair pulling, the close-ups of screaming girls in the balcony—and the suppressed squealing on the area rug by my cousins and me was enough to stop the card game in mid-deal and the cleanup of the dishes in mid-scrape.

"Lookit them Prince Valiant haircuts!" said my grandfather, his cigar permanently fixed in the corner of his mouth.

"Yeah, yeah, yeah? What the hell kind of lyrics are those?" said Uncle Jerry, anteing up.

"Those girls are all worked up. Over what?" said my mother, dripping dish suds on the floor.

Her feelings were hard to figure. On one hand, she liked to bond with us. Telling us stories about how much she and her sisters couldn't wait to hear the next record by Frank Sinatra. How they'd sit by the radio, eyes shut. Frankie! How her father had fits every time they'd bubble through the house with their socks rolled down, chattering about Frankie this and Frankie that. But, on the other hand, she was quick to chastise the saleslady over the fact that the photograph of the Beatles was larger than the one next to it, the one of "Our

Martyred President" on display in the record department in Gimbels. She'd sweep through our room, cleaning up, throwing away anything with the Fab Four on the cover.

My father revered John Wayne. Speaking against the Duke in our house was tantamount to blasphemy. Hysteria was not my father's style. His fan-ness manifested itself in a kind of subdued respect, like a soldier's for his commanding officer; that's how my dad gushed over John Wayne. He saw every one of his movies. Knew who the supporting cast members were. Could recite entire scenes of dialog. Anytime there was a John Wayne movie on TV, no matter how many times Dad had seen it, he watched it. The minute the credits rolled, that's where it ended. He didn't collect 8 x 10s of the Duke, or rip out magazine articles. Too girly.

We went everywhere with our transistor radios. We carried them in our bike baskets, to the park, to the library, tuned in to the *Bob Barry Show*. He was *the* DJ. Sort of Milwaukee's answer to Murray the K, only without the annoying jive. He always had the inside scoop on the Beatles. He knew about anything to do with them first, and then he passed it on to us, the fans.

All week long, the station had been teasing us about some big announcement. A new album? An exclusive interview? So we took our radios with us while we waited in line for the doors to the public pool to open. My batteries were going, and at first I missed the announcement. But someone in the back had turned a radio up way past distortion, and, despite the garbled voice, we could make out that the Beatles were coming to Milwaukee. What? *The Beatles are coming to the Arena on September 4! The Beatles are coming! The Beatles are coming!*

Who in their right mind could think about going swimming on a ninety-degree August afternoon? While the other kids in the pool were savoring the last swim before school started, my friends, my sister, and I sat in the changing area plotting.

Dad hadn't walked all the way into the kitchen. He was hot. He hadn't even taken off his gun belt. And he was crabby. All days off had been canceled. He'd have to give up his fishing trip. This whole Beatle thing was being treated like a visit from the president times ten.

My sister, noted for her lack of timing, asked to go (denied). She peppered him with options as he peeled off his sweaty uniform shirt. She tried using things in trade, like no allowance for six months, doing dishes for the rest of her life, picking up the dog poop without being nagged (denied, denied, denied). She tried logic: "Why can't I go?" And got the parental staple: "Because you're in my jurisdiction."

We couldn't look to my mother to see what she could do on this one. They were a united front. Ticket price wasn't an issue ($3.50, $4.50, and $5.50). Fear and foreboding on the part of my parents, especially my father—that was the issue. He had thought that this whole Beatle nonsense would be over by now, that they would just stay in England, make a few hits, get their money, and then go away. What was at first the bobbies' problem was becoming his problem. And he did not want to be worrying about the crowd and us at the same time. Who knows what could happen with twelve thousand emotionally charged adolescent girls? All hell could break loose. We wouldn't be setting foot near the Arena. Case closed.

B-Day, as it came to be known, finally arrived. It was a Friday. A school day. I identified with Cinderella as I watched Dad get ready for work. Holster, check. Gun, check. Billy club, check. Handcuffs, check. On a normal morning, our kitchen would be frenetic with activity. But, on this day, aside from the "tack, tack, tack" of the masking tape Dad used to get the lint off his uniform pants, the only other sound was the quiet scraping of my sister's spoon as she pushed her soggy cereal from one side of the bowl to the other, her head hung in despair.

Good teachers always use current events as an opportunity to educate, and my fourth grade nun, Sister Marcelline, was no exception. She used the Beatles' appearance to warn us throughout the day about worshiping false idols and giving into the sin of lust. When I went to deliver the lukewarm milk cartons to the upper grades, I noticed that there were a few empty desks that belonged to girls whose parents were obviously a lot more enlightened than mine. John, Paul, George, and Ringo were a bus ride away, and I was in school, trying not to disobey the Sixth Commandment.

The Beatles took the Arena's stage at 9:10 P.M. They opened with "I Saw Her Standing There." They played for thirty minutes! The newspaper reviewed the show, putting the words "concert" and "songs" in quotes. (After all, the reviewer said, they don't read music. All they do is play chords. And, according to John, he and Paul compose most of their songs by whistling at each other.)

There were stories of fans standing on the corner of Fourth and Kilbourn Avenues all night just to see whether they could catch a glimpse. Of girls walking to the concert from Kenosha and getting only as far as South Milwaukee before calling home. Of creative attempts to get into their hotel. (One kid pretended to be Ringo's brother. Too bad Ringo didn't have a brother.)

I went to bed, wishing that my dad had a different job. Why couldn't he work at Allen Bradley, or sell insurance, like everyone else's dad? Why did he have to be on the front lines all the time? Why couldn't he be bamboozled like other parents?

Saturday morning I got up early. Dad was already gone. Back to work. Ushering the Beatles out of town. On the table, alongside the cereal du jour, there were two small bars of soap, slightly used, the words "Coach House Inn" still legible. One book of matches with four missing. And a note from Dad, "From their room." *Aaaaaaahhhhhh!*

Forget the thing about me wanting him to have some desk job. Wait until Ann and Jean see these! No one else's dad comes home from work with something that might, just might, have been intimate with a Beatle.

Mob Mentality

My mother was the one who noticed the black sedan with two guys sitting in it parked down the block from our house. They had been there in the morning when she went out with my sister and me. And they were still there when we went out to play in the leaves that she raked into piles after lunch.

Maybe they were real estate agents looking at the house for sale on the corner. Or they could be salesmen ready to plow and plant the fertile turf of our subdivision.

But if the guys sitting in the car were salesmen, they weren't in a hurry to get out and make a sale. Maybe they had something to do with an incident that had happened a month earlier on an October evening.

It was one of those cold, wet evenings, and the rain was beginning to coagulate on the windshield. Dad was lucky enough to be cruising around the warehouse district in a heated squad instead of walking the beat weighed down by a heavy rubberized raincoat, popping in and out of doorways to wipe his face and readjust his hat. He hated walking the beat in the rain more than in the cold. You could always count on the warmth of a restaurant kitchen, long underwear, hunting socks, and constant movement to keep warm, but, once you were wet, you were wet.

He turned the corner and saw a light on in the second-floor window in one of the two-story brick buildings used by the commission merchants who bought and sold produce for the local grocery stores and restaurants. A light that shouldn't be on at 11:30 at night. And what about those cars parked in the alley? Hmmm. A late night crunching the numbers? Or maybe something else.

He doused the headlights of the squad, killed the engine, and coasted to a stop underneath a metal canopy that covered the loading dock. There was an unlucky copper walking the beat a block away. Dad motioned him over to the squad, telling him he suspected something was up.

They entered the cavernous building by the back door, conveniently left unlocked. Rats scurried behind the crates of yesterday's lettuce. The silhouettes of three, four, maybe five guys were visible behind the frosted glass panels of the office loft. Dad and the other copper could hear voices. "Shoot the ten!" "Awww, he faded!" "Go ahead, shoot!"

This was a full-scale crap game.

Dad and his sidekick crouched down and crawled up the makeshift steps built by somebody unfamiliar with a square and a level. He figured they could get a quick look at the layout of the room and then come up with a plan of attack, but the door to the office had easy hinges, and it swung open wider than it was supposed to. Surprise!

There were seven, maybe eight guys standing around a green felt–covered table piled with money, their cigarettes dangling from the corners of their mouths, their hats tipped back on their foreheads. "Get outta here! You ain't got no warrant!" one of them shouted. The others bolted out the window, rolling off the metal canopy onto the parked squad before scuttling down the slick, bricked alley. Dad managed to grab some dice and a ten-dollar bill before he and his partner subdued four of the men.

It was all over the papers. "Cops Bust In on Crap Game." Dad was interviewed. The relatives couldn't get enough. They called. They called back. They came over. There were mug shots in the paper of the four guys with their pencil-thin mustaches. They had those "Who, me?" kinds of expressions on their faces. According to them, "We wasn't doin' nothin'. Just talking business and stuff like dat." It was all so very Eliot Ness-y.

It was after the bust was reported in the paper that the black sedan appeared. Mom mentioned in passing that it always came after he left for work and was always gone by the time he got home. She would have mentioned it earlier, she really meant to, but she had forgotten about it—what with dinner, us kids, cleaning the house, and making sure Dad had an ironed shirt for the next day. That and thinking about how she was going to fit the relatives around the table for Thanksgiving dinner.

Dad phoned his shift commander. He suspected that this car and its two occupants had something to do with his ongoing investigation of the gambling ring. He had two kids and a wife at home during the day, and he wanted a police watch on the house. The commander thought he was being a little paranoid, that the men were probably salesmen scoping out the customers. He should be getting ready for work. They'd talk more about it after he reported for inspection.

Dad wasn't going to come into work. Not until he knew what those two guys were up to. He decided to do a field interview. He had just cause—they had been there in that same spot off and on for days in a big black Caddy in our Chevy station wagon kind of neighborhood.

He got his badge and his guns from the dresser when Mom reported from her chair in the living room that the two thugs were out of the car and coming toward the house.

"Get the kids and stay in the bedroom," Dad said, shoving his on-duty gun in the front pocket of his gray hooded sweatshirt and his small off-duty gun into his front pants pocket.

They rang the front doorbell and waited on the stoop. Nice and polite. One guy was small and had on a wide-brimmed hat pulled low over his eyes. He looked like a kid out for trick or treat, except that his five o'clock shadow hadn't been applied with a burnt cork. He chewed on a toothpick that was wedged between his front teeth. The other guy—some big galoot whose neck got lost between his chin and his chest—kept his hands in his pockets.

Dad recognized them. They were messengers trying to work their way up the crime ladder. Dad opened the front door and stepped out onto our stoop. He asked them what their business was in the neighborhood. They just wanted to know how things were at work. Did he ever have dreams of being a detective? They knew people who knew people who might be able to put in a good word. Dad said nothing. Then they wanted to know how things were with the wife. They might be able to get him some action on the side, if he was into that sort of thing. How was he doing with money? They knew a person couldn't afford the finer things in life on a cop's salary, and, since it was getting close to the holidays, maybe he could use some extra cash?

The big guy pulled out a wad of twenty-dollar bills. Dad slapped the guy's hand, and the bills went flying in the wind, mixing it up with our freshly raked maple leaves.

Okay. Okay. Not to worry. Not to worry. The little guy added emphasis with the chewed toothpick. They'd keep in touch.

Dad came back into the house, picked up the phone, and quickly kicked off the woman on the party line: "Official police business, ma'am." He spoke to his captain in that tone of voice that he used on my sister and me when he really meant business. First it was the voice, with a hint of a growl: "Hey, settle down!" Then he added a gesture—he'd point at us with his thick trigger finger: "I mean it!" Then, if we were still acting goofy, he'd unbuckle his belt and snap it at us. (Don't get me wrong, he never used the belt on us. Just the snap of it was enough for us to get back in line.) So now there was another black sedan parked in our neighborhood. But this one belonged to the good guys.

It wasn't until the gamblers were safely locked up that our lives got back to normal—no more big black cars in the neighborhood.

Dad was lying on his side on the couch, his head resting on his arm, and I was sitting in that triangular spot made by the bend in his legs. This was how we watched the *Bugs Bunny Show*. The scene cut away to two thugs, Rocky, a short guy—all fedora and toothpick—and his big neckless sidekick, Mugsy. Dad looked at me.

"Hey, those two guys . . . do they remind you of anybody?"

Cop Nabs Car Thief— Next Stop: The Slammer

Of all the newspaper articles that mentioned my father's name, this was my favorite headline. It was so Dick Tracy. My mother clipped the articles out of the *Milwaukee Journal* and the *Milwaukee Sentinel* and risked her office job by abusing the laminator to keep them fresh for posterity.

Whenever my father got his picture in the paper or had his name in print, I got special privileges at school and was the center of attention in the neighborhood until the novelty wore off.

The story about the car thief, the one with the snappy headline, didn't involve any high drama—no bodily harm, no weapons being drawn, just Dad being at the right place at the right time. After that one was in the paper, I got to pull down the big map of the United States for the entire day—a job normally given to Peggy Krueger, the straight-A student who never did anything wrong, but for one day, having a father that nabbed a car thief trumped scholastic achievement.

Then there was the story about two girls reported missing by their parents. One of their neighbors told Dad that she had seen the kids leaving in a taxi. Using his cop logic, Dad called the cab company and found out from the driver that they had been dropped off at the train station. Then he found out from the ticket seller at the train station that the two runaways had bought tickets to New York City. As they stepped off the train, New York police, reporters, and photographers greeted them. "Who told!" they whined. "Some cop back in Milwaukee." For that one, I got to go to the office and mimeograph the geography tests.

"Cop Foils Nude Dude." The benefits of that one were minor—just collecting the milk money and delivering it to the office. When I got home, I had to put up with the good-natured ribbing from the lady across the street: "I told my husband not to go driving around without a shirt—your father might arrest him!" I gave her a weak smile and a wave.

Any story that involved my father coming to the rescue of a puppy or some unfortunate waifs got me so many perks that it was embarrassing. Like the time there was a big picture on the front page of Dad holding a fifteen-month-old baby girl in one arm, with his other arm around her three-year-old brother. It was a classic photo, the warm-hearted cop engulfing the little

35

urchins in his protective embrace, gazing at them with a kind and gentle smile.

He had been called to the home by neighbors who had complained that the kids were left alone in the house without proper food or clothing. The girl weighed fifteen pounds with her blanket, and the boy had big welts on his back.

My friend Ann's mom let me sit in their kitchen and help myself to an orange popsicle. With eight kids, her mantra was, "Hey, I'm not feeding the world!" The only thing we could get out of her was a glass of water, maybe, in an actual glass. Otherwise, the garden hose would suffice.

Diane's mom didn't yell at me when I misjudged the turning radius of my roller skates and ended up going across her newly sealed patio and into the geraniums. Jean's mom wanted to know all the gory details: "Were the welts big and runny?" (I didn't know.) "Did the little girl's bones stick out?" (I didn't know.) Will we be adopting them? (What?)

There was another article about Dad busting up an underage drinking party at the Holiday Inn. Twenty-two kids in eight rooms. Dad and his cronies arrived, tipped off by a guest who had been disturbed by the noise, and put an end to the drunken debauchery. Sister Gregory let me open the classroom windows with the big hook for the entire week, even though it was Thomas Dombrowski's turn. We could all sleep better knowing that Dad had saved the world from a pack of wild, groping, drunken teens.

A picture of Dad at an accident scene, where the car was flipped over and the roof was crushed, was worth a thousand phone calls from all the relatives who didn't actually read the paper but just looked at the pictures.

If I was the first one to get to the phone, I had to answer questions like, "Did you see your father's picture in the paper?" "What did you think of your father's picture in the paper?" and "Are you going to save that picture of your father that was in the paper?" as if the aunt, cousin, uncle, or second cousin once removed from the first wife was the first one to ask me that question.

One time, there was a huge photo spread about a hostage situation involving a guy who had wounded a police officer and a paperboy. Photos of a cop unloading a volley of tear gas into the house. The Chief talking to the distraught mother of the suspect. Dad leaning against a telephone pole, listening intensely as the former hostages explained the layout of the house and the demeanor of the gunman. After several hours, the guy ended up surrendering.

Pretty impressive. Especially to my principal, Sister Mary Augusta. She summoned me to her office. Would I please take this message over to the convent for Sister Veronice? And, while I was there, I could help myself to a fresh nun-baked donut and a glass of milk.

Yep, sometimes this cop thing really did pay.

The Basement,
AKA the Rec Room

Every basement in our cul-de-sac masqueraded as something other than a basement.

The Nelsons' was a North Woods lodge. The walls were done in knotty pine paneling and accented with a Hamm's beer sign (the kind with the shimmering lake effect) and a large-mouth bass mounted on a piece of driftwood with a lure dangling uncomfortably close to its open mouth. (Poor fish. Imagine the one moment you wished you could take back, frozen in time, on display, forever.)

The Kopeckis turned their basement into a Polynesian paradise. The three steel support posts that ran the length of everyone's basement became palm trees. Mr. Kopecki built a cabana for the bar, with bamboo and thatching. Three walls were covered with fish netting and seashells. The other wall was a mural that Mrs. Kopecki painted to look like ocean waves crashing on the beach. The floor was painted to look like sand. It was the perfect setting for their *South Pacific* routine. It wasn't a party until either Mrs. Kopecki sang "I'm Gonna Wash That Man Right Out of My Hair" or Mr. Kopecki put on his grass skirt and coconut shells.

Mr. Hoffman spent the summer months in his garage with a chain saw carving bears, rabbits, and owls for his Black Forest motif. He covered the basement floor with wide pine planks. The support posts became tree trunks. Carved and painted trolls held up the bar. Wine skins and beer steins hung from the exposed rafters. Whenever the Hoffmans had a party, it was B.Y.O.L—bring your own lederhosen.

My father started turning our concrete block bunker of a basement into what was supposed to be a fun-filled family room on a weekend in March 1960. He had spent months on the phone switching days off, trading court time, and offering to fix gutters.

He had big plans. A laundry room, a workbench, a cedar closet for our winter coats and his deer hunting gear, a bar in the far corner with a built-in cubby for the hi-fi and enough room left over for a pool table? (Why not!) How about an extension phone? (Sure!) He worked without a plan on paper. ("It's all up here," he'd say, tapping his forehead with his finger.) Yeah, but what was it going to look like? An English manor house? The Ponderosa? I was worried. We had no theme.

He got all the framing done. Put in the recessed ceiling and the lights. Finished one whole wall of paneling.

Roughed in the spot for the closet and the bar. Then the phone rang. Grandma. There were two things that had the potential to put the kibosh on any plans. One: The Department. Two: Grandma.

Grandpa had fallen getting into the car. They had been on their way to play pinochle at Toots and Louie's, and Grandma had tried to lift him but felt a pain in her chest (The Big One?). He had better get over there and see what the hell was going on. Probably end up spending all evening at the hospital.

He called home around bedtime. Everything was fine. Grandpa had a badly bruised kneecap, and Grandma just had had a panic attack.

He came home late. He put away his tools, stacked the unused paneling between the one finished wall and the furnace, and corralled the sawhorses underneath the steps.

Oh, maybe he'd finish the family room on his next day off. Okay, probably as soon as he got back from fishing. But, then there was another emergency over at his mother's (she wanted the birdbath moved away from the statue of the Virgin Mary because Mary was getting pooped on). Then he'd pick up where he left off and have the rec room done for next Christmas. No, Easter—he promised. Definitely by the time I got married—it would be perfect for the shower. Uh huh. Every time he would drag out the sawhorses, the phone would ring. Grandma. Another emergency. It was uncanny. Did she have radar?

The Basement, AKA the Rec Room

We learned to work with what we had.

My mother used the header on the see-through closet to hang my father's uniform shirts after they came out of the dryer. Conduit was ideal for hanging her delicates—it didn't snag. Gaps in the two-by-four framing were great for stacking all those *National Geographic*s, boxes of shotgun shells, and the surplus rolls of toilet paper.

The unfinished walls were perfect for clipping up the bedsheet movie screen so that the First Communion procession didn't spill out onto the sofa and for my roller skating slalom course. My mother didn't worry about hanging pictures, either—if she didn't like the paint-by-number deer next to the bas-relief platter of fruit, she just yanked the nails out and started over.

The one paneled wall was the background for many a family photo op. Aunts, uncles, and cousins were arranged and rearranged on groups of mismatched folding chairs, babies blinking wildly, temporarily blinded by my father's movie lights.

When my parents had parties, Dad set the mood by replacing the regular bulbs in the ceiling lights with yellow ones. He used our old chrome kitchen table for the bar and the sanitary tubs for an ice bucket, and he stationed the quarter barrel near the floor drain.

The healthy stack of paneling slowly withered away. Sheets were extracted and made into doghouses, campers, and scenery. Eventually, my sister and I used them as a commodity. Boyfriends were made and kept with promises of perfectly good four-by-eight-foot sheets of paneling for van interiors and dorm room decorating.

The extension phone—big and black, with a plate-sized rotary dial—was finally installed months later. It hung on the wall in the supposed laundry room. We held many a private conversation while sitting on the washer during the spin cycle.

Eventually my father lugged our old television down there. He got an orange and green plaid sofa bed from somewhere. He made two end tables out of used ammo boxes. He had lamps made from his deer antler collection. Done. Our theme? Ed Gein meets Goodwill.

It worked for us.

Just Another Day at the Office

We were already up and getting ready for school. Mom was rushing around trying to do too many things at once: putting on lipstick, reminding us of what we were supposed to be doing instead of fighting over the morning paper, making the lunches, and rinsing off the breakfast dishes. She had to be at the bus stop by seven o'clock; otherwise, she'd be late. She worked downtown in a big office doing order entry. I never knew exactly what order entry was, but she did it with some other women named Regina, Beverly, and Darlene.

She slammed the medicine cabinet door and clomped around the linoleum in her high heels. She seemed crankier than usual. And she was making an awful racket. We were usually supposed to be quiet in the morning.

"Isn't Daddy sleeping?" I asked her while she wildly stirred the milk into her coffee.

"Your father isn't home from work . . . yet."

The latest he ever came home was around one o'clock in the morning, and he wasn't the kind of guy who went out after his shift to unwind either. Something was wrong.

Well, no word from his sergeant, or, worse, the captain. That's good. They're the ones who come to the house to tell the wife about the shooting, and how the Department will be adding her husband's name to the wall of honor for giving his life in the line of duty, but she shouldn't worry because she'll be getting widow's benefits.

My sister spotted the reason for Dad's absence. There was an article buried in the morning paper's main news section, page twenty-four: "Kid Confesses to Coppers."

An eighteen-year-old kid had been arrested after fighting with my father on the street. He was wanted in the connection with the beating death of an old man, as well as for beating the crap out of two other people. Wow. Dad in a fight? I wondered whether it had been like it was on television, only without the musical score. Had this kid tried to do to Dad what he had done to three other people that night? Was Dad okay?

Mom agonized out loud. "Should I call in sick? I've got no paid sick days left." She rubbed her temples with her fingertips. Was she talking to me? Was I supposed to answer her? Offer her my opinion? "No. I'll go in. Your father would want me to," she said, straightening up from the kitchen counter. She looked at the clock. "No, I'll call in . . . I mean, how will I be able to concentrate, worrying whether or not your father is lying in a hospital emergency room somewhere calling my name?"

She walked over to the phone chair. Sat down and dialed the number. "Darlene, I'm not coming in today . . . there's an emergency here at home . . . well, just give my pile to Reg, she's usually staring into space by two-thirty . . . I know, well, you'll just have to dock me, then."

Too bad. We still had to go to school.

Sister Gregory was extra nice to me all day. I got to pass out the mimeographed tests (take in a few whiffs) and collect the milk money. She asked me how Dad was; I told her I didn't know, that he hadn't come home from work yet. She said that she would remember him in her prayers, and she gave me a squeeze. I hadn't been all that worried about Dad until I started getting all this attention. Stuff like this happened to the other kids when someone died. Did she know something that I didn't?

I thought of what it would be like for us without Dad. Would Mom be another Jackie? Would I be another John-John saluting the flag-draped casket as it went by? Who would take us fishing? Mom? She couldn't even pull the cord for the motor. What would Christmas be like? Uncle Jerry would have no one to exchange twenty-dollar bills with. Who would Grandma call to spackle and paint her hallway? She'd have to pay someone to do it. I suppose I'd have to be the man in the family.

How long would it be before the sympathy wore off? When someone's grandparent died, that was good for at least a week, not including the days off from school for the funeral. But this—this would have to be bigger than a grandparent. I mean . . . he wasn't even old. And it was in the line of duty! That would have to be good for a month. And then it would be business as usual; I'd be back to getting yelled at for making the class laugh when Sister was trying to explain the mystery of the Immaculate Conception.

Would Mom get remarried? To whom? Not that guy she was always complaining about—Mr. Sanfillipo—the guy who leaned over her desk a little too far. Or what about that one guy that lived up the block—the guy who always gave out good Halloween candy, the one with the boat and the camper? I think he was a lawyer. Not bad looking. But I think he was divorced, and that wouldn't go over with the Catholic Church.

The dismissal bell rang.

I didn't want to go home for two reasons.

Number one: What if Dad still wasn't home? There were times when he had changed and left for work again before we got home. He'd leave a little note on the table with our instructions for the afternoon: "Peel the spuds. Make the coffee. Set the table. Dad." What if this wasn't one of those times? I was afraid Mom would still be sitting in the rocker, a damp Kleenex in her hand, the house in the same state it had been in when we left for school. She'd call us over and give us the bad news.

Number two: We were supposed to be driven home by Muriel Dombrowski. She was the mother of Dean and Dawn, two kids in the upper grades who lived around the block from us. She was a small, bird-like woman with a tight perm and rhinestone glasses on a silver chain. She drove an old, round, two-toned Buick that coughed blue smoke out of the tail pipe. Muriel gripped the platter-size steering wheel as if she were afraid it would get away. She knew only how to accelerate and then come to an abrupt stop. We were tossed around in the back seat like the crew in *Voyage to the Bottom of the Sea* when a mutant sea creature from some Russian nuclear accident was attacking the sub. I felt a lot safer when there were more kids in the car because then I could wedge myself between two seventh-graders.

Muriel gunned into her driveway and hit the brakes. I lurched forward, hitting my head on the back of the front seat. My book bag was tossed out of my lap, and papers spilled over the hump on the floor. Muriel came around to my door. "Hey, I heard about your dad." She shook her head but offered no other information. "Make sure you shut the door when you're done." She turned and followed Dean and Dawn through their back door.

I took the short cut through the back of the Kufels' garage and the Kopeckis' yard.

47

I opened our kitchen door and smelled Mr. Clean. The house was spotless. There were chocolate chip cookies piled on a brown paper bag on the counter next to the stove. Was that a pot roast I smelled in the oven?

Dad was in the rocker reading the afternoon paper. He had his slippers and his chinos on.

"Hey, how was school?" he said, putting down the paper. He had a welt above his left eye and a few scratches on his cheek. I'd never seen the results of a fight. On television, guys got beat up all the time, but there was never any swelling.

"Okay. Hey, how was your day?" I asked.

He looked at Mom, who was sitting on the sofa, fixing the tears in his uniform overcoat.

"Oh, just another day at the office."

The Banana Incident

Police Department regulations stipulated that no employee could engage in any other work for hire while employed as a Milwaukee police officer. But a lot of guys did, including my father.

Dad came from that generation where the man went to work and brought home the paycheck, and the wife stayed home with the kids and made do, which they did. They rented an apartment—a converted attic—in Dad's Uncle Joe's house, with a kitchen conveniently located three flights down in the basement. Well, it was close to the bus stop, and Dad could ride to work for free if he was in uniform.

There were new houses being built all over the city—but what about the down payment? Gotta save. Gotta make do. Gotta have a side job.

So, Dad got a little job delivering flowers for his cousin's husband's friend. He'd deliver only to customers outside the city limits. He figured that way he was safe—because all police personnel had to live within the city. The other advantage to this caper was that Dad had access to a car with a seat that folded down, and he was going to get mileage on top of it.

It was Mother's Day weekend. The back seat was full of boxes and centerpieces. "To Mother, with love." "For you, Mom, on your special day." "We love you, Mom!" Everything was destined for cherished mothers in Brookfield, Waukesha, and Hales Corners. Except for the last box.

Dad took a look-see at the address. It wasn't familiar, but the name on the card was. Mrs. Edward Davis. Well, Davis is a common name, and Edward, well, there are thousands of Edwards. What were the chances of this Mrs. Edward Davis being the wife of Sergeant Edward Davis, Dad's immediate superior officer? Dad bounded up the walkway and rang the bell. The Edward Davis who opened the front was indeed his sergeant.

"Here, I believe these are for your lovely wife," Dad said, thrusting the box into the hands of his surprised superior, exiting before the sergeant had a chance to put two and two together.

At roll call the next day, Dad waited for the sarge to say something. Dad figured he would have to play on the sarge's sympathy. Work in the fact that there was a baby on the way, but nothing happened. Phew! He had dodged that bullet.

Another side job that Dad had was with a guy who had seen his share of troubles with the law but was a good egg and was trying to make a go of it with his own house painting business. Dad helped him out with the painting and varnishing when he could. It wasn't bad work, and he learned a few tricks along the way (which he has since regretted, because any relative who needs something painted, Dad gets called in for spackling and priming duty).

He was called in to help with a big job in Fox Point. It was in one of those huge mansions that were built in the 1920s by some rich industrialist. Cherry moldings and raised paneling in the upstairs bedrooms. Bird's-eye maple in the master suite. Oak, butternut, and mahogany throughout the first floor. There was a library. A butler's pantry. The kitchen was bigger than the cheesy flat in Uncle Joe's place. Boy. This was nice!

Dad was busy kneeling on the floor, varnishing the molding, concentrating on not getting anything on the freshly painted wall (even though there was masking tape, he liked to challenge himself to not even get anything on the tape). Every few feet, he'd have to readjust, move his drop cloth, and straighten his back. That's when he saw the other guy out on the lawn clipping the hedges. Mike Klobonski. A fireman. They shared an I-won't-tell-if-you-won't look.

There was always the risk that somebody would play by the book instead of the unwritten rules. So far, Dad had been lucky—until the banana incident.

Dad's beat was in Milwaukee's Third Ward, where the commission merchants bought and sold produce.

Usually the trucks came in at four or five in the morning, but this one—loaded with bananas—was really early, backing into the dock at midnight. The weather was hot and humid, and a truckload of bananas would start to turn if it wasn't unloaded quickly.

Most of the guys who worked on the dock came by way of the Rescue Mission, but on this particular night, they were fresh out of recent converts to sobriety. Hey, would Dad mind helping? The banana man had some old clothes he could wear. He could change right in the office. Nobody would know. A couple hours at the most. Good money. Cash.

12:00 P.M.: Dad calls Mom. She has trained herself to answer the phone on the first ring regardless of how deep her REM sleep is. It's the end of his shift. He tells her not to worry. He'll be a little late. Okay, she'll see him later when he gets home.

12:30 P.M.: He arrives at the loading dock, having walked from District Number One (police headquarters in downtown Milwaukee), and is changed and ready for the unloading.

2:15 A.M.: Mom expects to feel the warm lump of a snoring husband next to her by now. Where is he? Maybe Jerry, his brother, would know.

2:20 A.M.: She calls Jerry. He says not to worry. That Dad is probably at the station filling out reports. You know what a lousy typist he is. Besides, if it's anything bad, The Department will get in touch with her, so go back to sleep.

2:25 A.M.–3:45 A.M.: Mom starts to think of all kinds of scenarios. Maybe Dad is locked up in one of those warehouses and needs help. She pictures him with a gaping head wound trying to crawl across a produce littered floor. Go . . . toward . . . light . . . must . . . get . . . back . . . to . . . wife. What if somebody has him tied to a chair? He'll be left to rot like so many cantaloupes. No one will ever find him.

3:50 A.M.: Mom is convinced that Dad is missing in action. She calls the station and asks to speak to his sergeant. Sergeant Davis. She remembers him. She had met him at some of the policeman's picnics. He's the type of guy who likes to be in charge, plays by the rules, and puts people on the spot. Not in a fun way, where everyone laughs. More like in a way that shows everyone who's the boss. But, his wife is nice, kind of quiet.

4:00 A.M.: While Mom waits for the sergeant to pick up the phone, she's picturing herself a hero for notifying his superiors—"Thank God your wife called; otherwise we would never have known you were in there!" There's a photo in the paper of the two of them, reunited, Mom giving Dad a kiss on his sticky cheek.

4:05 A.M.: Sergeant Davis tells her he doesn't know where Dad is. But he'll check around the station.

4:45 A.M.: The phone rings. It's Dad's sergeant. He tells Mom that everyone he has talked to has said that they saw Dad filling out some reports and that he had left the building at the end of his shift. The sarge didn't think that Dad was the kind of guy that fooled around.

He begins to think that maybe the incident with the flowers wasn't a one-time occurrence. He tells Mom that he will be over to ask her a few questions.

5:15 A.M.: The sarge comes by the house. He looks around. Hmmm. Brand-new television in the living room, new portable radio on the counter, a Mixmaster, an electric coffee pot. Hmmmmm.

"Does your husband do this kind of thing often?"

"What kind of thing?" Mom doesn't like his tone.

He checks out their "kitchen"—a folding table with a coffeepot and a radio. "Is that one of them new electric percolators? Gee, my wife wants one of those, but aren't they expensive? Just where did you get that one? Did your husband surprise you with it?"

"Well, he picked it up on his way home."

"Uh huh." The sarge makes a note in his little brown book.

The cagey old dog puts two and two together. This young cop, on the job for three years, is doing side jobs to buy the finer things in life for the little woman. An electric coffee pot! A television! Why, when he was first on the job, they had to live with his parents for ten years and put up with all the questions: "So? When are you going to have a baby?" And what is wrong with listening to the radio? There's *Dragnet. This Is Your F.B.I. Crimebusters.* What the hell do you want with a TV? This young upstart needs a lesson. "Don't worry. I'll find him."

Mom stands at the top of the stairs, nervously playing with the buttons on her housecoat, while the sergeant clomps down the two flights and leaves.

She hopes that she did the right thing.

5:45 A.M.: Dad is on the loading dock knee deep in bananas when the sergeant, cruising by in his squad, spots him. Dad ducks behind some crates.

The sarge wants to know who's in charge and who all is working here? He's looking for a guy, about twenty-five years old, blond, thin build. He wants to bring the guy in for some questioning. Has anybody seen a guy like that? One of the winos points to a bunch of crates. The jig is up.

"He was just helping us out," the banana man says. "He wasn't getting any money. He was just doing us a favor. He's never done this before!"

The sarge listens with his head cocked to one side.

"Never done anything like this before? What about making deliveries? On Mother's Day weekend?"

The sarge ordered Dad to change back into his uniform. He drove him back to the station, in cuffs, in the back seat of the squad. Dad's stomach did a turn. He figured his ass was grass. He'd have to start all over. He'd have to go back to the foundry taking the molds out of the blast furnace. Maybe it wouldn't be so bad. Maybe he wouldn't break out in those boils like he did before.

The sarge pulled the squad into the garage and into farthest space from the radio shack. He started giving Dad the third degree. "What were you doing at that loading dock? Getting paid to unload those bananas? I suppose you do this kind of thing all the time? You better come clean with me, kid. I know it was you delivering those flowers. What else you been doing? And for what? You think you gotta buy all that stuff for the wife! The gadgets. That's the trouble with you young guys. Gotta have all this new stuff. Well? What have you got to say?"

Dad's tongue stuck to the roof of his mouth.

"Alls I have to do is write this up and you're done for. You know that?"

"Well, it wouldn't be so bad if it was just her and me, but with the baby on the way . . . " Dad hated to play this card. He knew that the sarge and his wife had tried for years to have kids, that she had gotten pregnant many times and had lost the baby.

The sarge took a breath and exhaled through his nose. It made a whistling sound.

"Okay. I'm not writing the report. But, I'm not lettin' you get off easy. I'm assigning you to election duty. Report to work in fifteen minutes."

On election day, each polling place had a police officer assigned to it. When the polls opened at 7:30 A.M., the police officer went outside and yelled, in a town crier fashion, "Oy yea, Oy yea, the (insert aldermanic ward number here) aldermanic ward is now open for voting!" and then the officer went inside to maintain order. When the polls closed at 8:00 P.M., the police officer stood at the end of the line so that no one could come in after the official polling hours and then announced, again using the town crier method, that the polling place was now closed for official business.

It was Dad's duty to take the ballots and the paperwork to the city hall for tabulation—completing a twenty-eight hour shift.

Ever since the sergeant had left their shabby (but clean) attic rooms, my mother had been wringing her hands. She didn't like his tone of voice. It had an air of suspicion about it. Along with an I've-seen-it-all-before kind of attitude. What had she done? What trouble had she gotten Dad into? How would she ever face him? She did what any good Catholic woman in turmoil would have done—she got dressed and went to church.

"Lord, please don't let them fire him. I swear that if my husband comes home with his job intact, I'll never ever ever jump to any conclusions again. And (as a bonus) I'll never think bad thoughts about my mother-in-law ever again. Ever never ever! Amen."

She sat there most of the day, using up all her bus fare to light the vigil lights. Dad saw her coming out of the church just as he was getting off the bus. He had a large envelope under his arm full of polling material and no badge pinned to his shirt. He was dog-tired. Mom ran up to him. "Where's your badge?" She began

57

to cry. In a "Whhaaaaaaaaa!" Lucy Ricardo way. He could have put his arm around her shoulder and given her a there-there squeeze and then explained that everything was okay, but he really didn't feel like talking. He'd rather just try and forget the past twenty-eight hours—the acid stomach, the humiliation. He'd just let her think they fired him until they got home; then he'd pull the badge out of his pocket and have dinner.

The Payoff

Dad got paid every other week on Thursday. If he wasn't working and I didn't have school (because of some holy day or teacher's convention), I'd get to go downtown with him to pick up his check.

We'd have to go to the Safety Building—the big police headquarters. It was near all the legal action—down the block from the courthouse, next door to the jail. We'd park underground, in the police parking garage. Dad always found a spot near the wall, right next to the cars with the big "evidence" stickers on their windows.

The office doors had names painted in big black letters on the frosted glass. "Arson," "Vice," "Narcotics," "Robbery." Men and women, some in uniform, some in civilian clothes, walked in and out of offices carrying files and chatted in the hallways with guns nonchalantly attached to their hips or tucked away in shoulder holsters. Very *Man from U.N.C.L.E.*

The Payoff

We took the elevator to the floor where payroll was, but it wasn't the same elevator that the general public took. It was marked "Police Personnel Only." Dad had a special key to gain access. He would let me push the button for the ninth floor, and then he and I would move to the back of the car.

Other cops would get on, some in uniform. Dad told me that the ones who weren't in uniform, the ones in the nice suits, were the detectives. When one of them recognized Dad, they'd talk about stuff, sometimes about a case that they were working on. I heard words I never knew before, like hooker and pimp, zip gun, and junkie. They'd talk about making a bust soon. They'd say that all the overtime Dad put in was going to pay off. That his undercover work was going to earn somebody a long stay in The Big House. I didn't know that Dad was working undercover! So that's why he was driving my grandparent's car and going to work in his painting pants and fishing shirt.

Some of the detectives would ask my dad what kind of trouble I'd gotten into. Larceny? Disorderly conduct? Dad would join in the joke, saying he was taking me upstairs to be fingerprinted.

On the seventh floor, the doors opened, and some gray-haired grandpa type got on. All the witty banter stopped. Everyone stood a little straighter. They saluted him. It was The Chief.

In our house, there were four names that one uttered with respect and reverence: President Kennedy,

Vince Lombardi, Pope John XXIII, and Harold Breier (sometimes referred to simply as H. B.). Chief Breier was an amalgam of the other three men. He looked a little bit like Pope John XXIII—like a bulldog. He had the demeanor of Vince Lombardi—no-nonsense, gruff, and to the point. And he had the celebrity of JFK. According to Dad, it was Harold Brier who saved the Department from turning into a politically driven bureaucratic hellhole.

H. B. looked around the elevator and spotted me, a nine-year-old girl in a Notre Dame sweatshirt, jeans with iron-on patches at the knees, and red plaid Keds. He gave me a little wink, patted me on the head, and got off on eight. The guys all congratulated me. Dad beamed.

Payroll was full of office girls with very high hair and tight skirts all giving my dad a hard time about where he was going to spend all this money ($95 for two weeks of laying his life on the line) and how I'd better keep my eye on him. Dad's ears turned red.

We'd bump into Uncle Jerry, who worked in the Personnel Department across the hall. He and Dad would lean up against the two-toned green wall, dark olive drab on the bottom and a sicker, lighter green on the top. (Wasn't that the same color as our basement walls?) They'd talk about who was getting promoted, who wasn't, and who was in trouble with the shift commander, and close with who was going to run the family picnic next July. All the while, Uncle Jerry would be flicking his spent cigar ashes into someone's personnel file.

The elevator ride down wasn't as exciting as the ride up, unless we stopped at the fourth floor and the prisoners got on. They'd be shackled at the wrists and led in by two burly sheriff's deputies. Dad would place his hands on my shoulders and pull me back against his legs. There wasn't much these guys could do. The deputies warned the men not to talk, but once, this small skinny guy with greasy gray hair and facial stubble recognized my dad.

"Hey, Mark the Cop?"

"Hey, Leo! How's it goin'?" Dad extended his hand to give Leo's a hearty shake. Leo attempted to meet his, but they both stopped midway, realizing the shackle problem.

"Well, not too bad. And you?"

"Pretty good, pretty good."

Leo was Dad's Otis, the town drunk on *The Andy Griffith Show*. While walking the beat near Commission Row, the place near the Milwaukee River with all the warehouses where the vendors came to sell and buy produce, Dad had heard someone calling for help. Where was it coming from? He went up and down the block looking underneath the loading docks with his flashlight—nothing. Still the unmistakable cry for help continued. It was coming from inside one of the big barrels next to a pile of lettuce crates. There was Leo, inside, folded in half. Dad used his billy club to break the stiles, and, as if he were delivering a baby, he grabbed Leo by the head and pulled him out.

The elevator doors slid open on one. The deputies led the line of men out, their chains chinkling down the hall.

"Hey, Leo, stay out of trouble!" Dad shouted. Leo gave him a nod.

Next stop, the bank. We'd pull into the underground drive-up window, the only one I had ever seen. At the other bank, in the shopping center near our house, Dad had to park the car and go inside and wait in line; it always took too long, and there was nothing for me to do. I thought this bank was very Jetson-y, the way Dad put the check in the little tube, and with the push of a button it was whooshed away.

The woman in the booth looked green from the overhead fluorescent lighting and the thick bulletproof glass that separated her from the customers. Her sweater was held on by a chain clipped to the top button, the sleeves dangling free while she quickly flipped through the money. When she sent back the tube, sometimes there was a tootsie roll in it. She'd sign off by saying, "See you in two weeks!" or "Don't spend it all in one place!"

Too bad we didn't listen to her. After the bank, it was on to the grocery store. And, if there was anything left, and Dad made sure there was, he would treat himself and me to Leon's frozen custard.

Loaded Questions

"I wouldn't want to be chasing someone down a dark alley without my two friends, Smith and Wesson," Dad would say to me every time he cleaned his service revolvers. I loved watching my father clean them. His on-duty gun was a .38-caliber model M-5 Smith and Wesson. His off-duty gun was a .38-caliber snub-nosed Smith and Wesson.

He'd spread the newspaper out across the kitchen table and lay out the equipment: the long thin rod with the clip on the end, the two-inch flannel squares, the tiny brushes, the bottle of Hoppe's No. 9 lead solvent. Everything had to be organized like surgical instruments before a tricky operation.

He'd dismantle his guns one at a time, and then he'd start with the cleaning. He'd do the smaller .38 first. He'd unload it, handing me the bullets. They were so cute! Like little golden Barbie bombs. I'd arrange them with the pointy tips up along the newspaper columns to form a shiny stockade.

It was my job to squirt the Hoppe's on the center of one of the flannel squares (making sure I got a little whiff—like the mimeographed tests in school, I couldn't resist the fumes) and load it on the tip of the long metal rod. Dad would eyeball the inside of the barrel, his tongue folded and clenched between his teeth (a sign of intense concentration), and push the flannel into it until it popped out the business end (as he called it).

It needed to be reloaded with another square and a squirt of Hoppe's until the flannel came out clean. He'd give me pointers. "Always clean the weapon in the same direction that the bullet travels. You wouldn't want to pull a dirty patch back through the bore of the gun; it would defeat the purpose."

Dad would insert the rod three, four, maybe five times, lecturing me on the proper use of the weapon. It wasn't a toy. I must never pick it up unless he told me to, and *never ever* point it at anyone.

The guns had no appeal to me. They were dark, dull, and heavy. I was into Barbies. If the guns were pink plastic and came with accessories, and the bullets had tips covered with purple daisies, well, then I might have been tempted.

The chambers in each of the barrels had to be cleaned with a tiny little brush, which was the only thing that could get the tangles out of Midge's hair without destroying her perky flip. Dad replaced the barrel on the snub-nosed .38 and spun it, and, with a flick of his wrist, it clicked back into position.

This was the gun that I'd seen many times. Sitting on the kitchen counter next to the cookie jar, sometimes on the table underneath the bills or in a holster hanging in Dad's closet next to one of his two belts.

The only time I touched it was when he'd remember that he'd left it in the car. He'd be settling into the sofa, ready to watch an evening of TV. I'd be on the floor with my bowl of potato chips and my glass of Squirt watching the Kraft commercial. Just as the well-manicured hands were about to dump in the whole bag of Kraft miniature marshmallows into the tuna casserole, this sleepy voice would come down from the sofa: "Would you go and get my gun from the car?"

I would dutifully go and retrieve the potentially lethal piece of hardware, carrying it at arm's length, like a foul-smelling diaper.

The Police Department's regulations stated that an officer was required to carry a weapon with him at all times, on duty and off. Dad claimed he was never off duty, that he was always on the lookout for bad guys, whether at the grocery store or at a wedding.

Every summer, we'd have a big family picnic at Greenfield Park. There were relatives there I had never even known I had and some I wished I didn't have—like Uncle Heinie with the green teeth and the Wolfman hairline. Dad always got roped into cooking.

Loaded Questions

He was supposed to be keeping an eye on the bur-
gers, but, one time, he was eyeballing a guy who was
hanging around the lagoon. "Get my gun out of the
glove compartment," he side-mouthed to my mother.
Trouble. Anytime he said that, or "Get my badge from
the dresser," there was going to be trouble.

Dad traded my mother the spatula for the handgun
and quickly walked over to the guy, who was sitting on
the rocks, not really doing much. They looked like they
were engaging in friendly conversation, Dad leaning
against a tree, still wearing the apron that said "Well
Done" across the chest, a plaid hot pad folded and
stuffed into his back pocket. And then, Dad flashed his
badge and exposed the holstered gun underneath the
ketchup-stained apron. Whatever the guy was up to, he
stopped it and left the park. Dad came back, said nothing, relieved Mom of her cooking detail, and turned
the hot dogs. Come and get it!

I tried to listen in on the adults talking about what
had happened, but if I got too close, they'd clear their
throats and chew in silence.

Dad was never flashy about carrying his gun, prefer-
ring to keep it out of sight, in a holster around his waist
covered up by an untucked shirt. I got pretty good at
recognizing off-duty cops by their bulges.

But my Uncle Jerry was different. Maybe it was because he worked in the personnel office, handling
background checks on new employees. Not much
chance of chasing a felon down a dark alley, just of

chasing paperwork down a dark file cabinet drawer. He wore his gun everywhere. He used to mow his lawn in his swimming trunks, with his gun in a shoulder holster. Sometimes a concerned citizen would call the police on him, saying there was an armed man in the neighborhood. The squad would show up. The officers would pop out with their weapons drawn. Jerry would have to turn off the Lawn Boy, explain that he was a police officer, and yell for my Aunt Effie to get his badge off of his dresser, and everyone would have a good laugh.

There were times when Dad delegated the weapons detail to my mother. If I needed a Kleenex, I always asked permission before I went rummaging through her purse. I never knew whether she would be packing heat.

Dad's on-duty gun was bigger. It had a fake pearl handle, like the six-shooter John Wayne strapped across his hip. This one took more time and flannel to clean. I coveted those cream-colored squares because they made great quilts for my dolls. I'd sew them together on my pink Kenner sewing machine. If there were enough, Barbie and Ken would get matching winter coats!

I asked Dad questions while he concentrated. I could tell he was really focusing because not only was he folding and unfolding his tongue between his teeth, but also he was switching his tongue from side to side.

"Dad, did you ever have to shoot someone?"

"No . . . (tongue switch). But I've taken my gun out of the holster and had to point it at someone."

"Did you ever get shot at?"

"Yes, several times."

"Weren't you scared?"

"No . . . (tongue switch). There's a lot that goes through your mind. You don't have time to be scared."

"Did you ever have to conk somebody on the head with the end of your gun? Like they do on TV?"

"No, and I wouldn't want to."

"Why not?"

"Because that wouldn't be the proper use of the equipment."

As Dad reassembled the service revolver, I disassembled my stockade, gave him back all the bullets, and wiped off the tools. He put all the oily newspaper outside on the back stoop and all the blackened squares into the metal garbage can. For my trouble, Dad slipped me a few clean flannel squares. Barbie would be getting a new coat this fall!

Games That Cops Play

The hubbub started in January when the vacation schedule was passed around. The guys of the District Number One early shift bugged Dad: "When's the picnic this year?"

Everyone wanted to go. But only two-thirds of the shift would be allowed to have the day off. The department wouldn't compromise the safety of the citizenry for the sake of a picnic. Dad didn't have to worry about it because he worked in the Juvenile Division. He was in charge of the kid games and buying prizes. Narcotics and Vice brought the beer. Homicide brought the meat.

The picnic was held outside everyone's jurisdiction at Regner Park in West Bend because the guys just wanted to spend a nice afternoon catching up on office gossip and playing softball without worrying about whether or not the people near the pavilion had any outstanding warrants.

It gave the wives a chance to talk to one another while the kids were busy playing Pin-the-Tail-on-the-Suspect and the Chalk Outline Game or tested their skill at the water-pistol firing range.

"He got home late because he had to jump into the Milwaukee River to fish a guy out, and then he had to go to the hospital for a tetanus shot. I'm telling you I tried everything, but I can't get that rotten fish smell out of his shirt."

"You know, my husband tells me that he can be the first guy to pry somebody out of a mangled car, or find a body that's been in a dumpster for over a week, but nothing turns his stomach more than the sight of a kid with a runny nose." They all laughed.

The best part of the day was after lunch, when the grown-ups played egg toss. Two lines formed. A husband across from a wife, six feet apart. Dad used two wash lines on the grass for a foul line, in accordance with the International Egg Toss Rules and Regulations for 1963.

Dad would go up and down the line handing one fresh egg to each wife, who had been coached during lunch by her husband to remove all rings and to pitch pop-ups, not fastballs. I couldn't wait to get married. At ten years old, that's how I was going to pick a mate, by his egg toss ability.

The first toss was easy. A few drops. No breaks. A few terse remarks from the catchers reminding the wives about technique: "Just like we practiced on the lawn, honey!"

Two giant steps backward. On the count of three, the husbands lofted three dozen white ovoids in graceful arcs.

The woman with the red ponytail misjudged her egg's downward trajectory. "Got yourself one a them egg shampoos, Vivian!" She walked toward the water pump trying to shake off the slimy goo.

Two more giant steps backward. The judges called time while the foul lines were stretched and reset.

What the women lacked in accuracy, the husbands made up in technique. One guy in Romeo slippers and plaid Bermuda shorts made a major league catch. The guy next to him, with a lot more belly under his belt, wasn't so lucky. He walked off the field, picking egg-shell out of his navel. He told his wife he had been sure that this was going to be their year. The guy with the red crew cut backpedaled toward the parking lot. His egg landed on the gravel but didn't break. Cries of "Hard-boiled!!" rose out of the gallery.

After three more tosses, the winning couple, the captain and his wife, walked off the yolk-soaked playing field with a two-pound canned ham.

Next up? The tug of war.

The troops assembled in the field next to the baseball diamond—the grizzled veterans, the young rookies, the ranking officers, the patrolmen. The only guy who didn't participate was the guy everybody called Mother Hanner.

He was a ten-year veteran who worked in the office tabulating how many tickets and arrests each officer had each month. He never walked a beat. He never drove in a squad. He admitted that he would rather have a root canal without Novocain than be out there. His claims to fame were his record keeping, his sewing skills, and his baking. When Mother baked, the dispatcher sent out an all-points bulletin. Squads screamed into the First District Station from all areas of the city. Crime would wait. The pecan crescents wouldn't.

When Dad pulled the coil of two-inch-thick jute rope from our station wagon, the rear springs gave a sigh of relief. Mother Hanner assigned each side a captain. The sides were picked. If there was too much beef on one, it was up to Mother to make things right.

Strategy was decided. Each team dug in. Mother blew the whistle. Muscles strained. The other side got the leverage. It was over in less than a minute. Some members of the losing side questioned the lay of the land. They complained that they had to pull uphill. Mother stepped in. "How about the best two out of three?" Agreed.

The teams switched sides, but the results were the same. Dad's team was not going to walk away with any two-pound canned hams, not this year.

There was time before supper for the kids to play

Find the Clues at the Crime Scene, sort of a cop version of a scavenger hunt. Kids got to keep all the evidence that they found — candy cigarettes, a trick knife, fake diamond rings, a rubber hatchet, a cap gun.

After all the coals were reduced to gray powder and all the canned hams were given away, there was one more event left. It wasn't a game so much as it was a ritual — trying to jump across the narrow creek that ran behind our picnic area.

Regner Park had a cold spring that bubbled up near Picnic Area Seven. It came up from a sandy spot and ran down a stream that fed into a lagoon and then flowed into the creek. People stuck their watermelons and six-packs in it to keep them cold.

During the day, I'd see guys scoping out the prime spots for takeoff. They'd walk around testing the firmness of the bank, seeing where the reeds weren't too high, where the rocks didn't get too slimy.

This was not a sanctioned event, so Mother Hanner was not called to duty. He sat tsk-tsking, shaking his head with the wives, trading recipes between attempts.

Dad never participated. I kind of wanted him to, but only if he would be the only one to clear the bank and land well beyond the reeds on the other side, like some Olympic pole vaulter. I didn't want to see him come up from the bottom with an algae hairpiece.

Dad and I sat on top of the picnic table and hooted and hollered with the rest of the crowd, watching the guys take a running start, get over the reeds, fall short of the opposite bank, and splash into the water, then slip up the bank, their pants all mucky from the creek bed.

When the diehards started stripping down to their underwear for their fourth attempt and the mosquitoes became unbearable, that was our cue to pack up the car and head home.

Five Minutes and Counting

There was nothing more contentious in our house than the use of the telephone. The phone was not for idle conversation about the mundane aspects of the day's events or for catching up on family gossip. It was a conduit for police communications.

After living in my militantly Polish grandmother's attic, in the shadow of St. Josaphat's Basilica on Milwaukee's south side, for the first year of their marriage, then in their own apartment in Uncle Joe's upper flat, my parents built their dream home. Dad was happy because it had a driveway. No more trying to find a parking space for his used 1938 Plymouth, and no more alleys to shovel. My mother was happy because she had escaped the overbearing eye of her mother-in-law, not to mention the smell of cooked cabbage and liver.

When my parents moved into their new two-bedroom Shangri-la in 1955, my Dad had been on The

Job for four years. My father's work was always referred to as The Job, as in "He's not on The Job anymore. He's selling Chevrolets." Or, "The Job got to be too much for his wife to handle. She took the kids and left him."

One of the first things they did was have a telephone installed. My mother had grown up without one. My father's family was considered well off. Not only did they have a car when he was growing up, but they also had a phone.

Our first phone line was a party line. That didn't last long. My dad thought it was going to save money, but when the sergeant tried to get hold of him, he didn't want to hear about some woman's husband's vein stripping or the recipe for Baker's dry cottage cheese torte (wasn't it on the back of the container?) every time he picked up the receiver. So we got a limited line.

We were allowed ten outgoing calls per week and unlimited incoming calls. This worked out okay for the first ten years—until my sister and I hit our teens.

You know that scene from the movie *Bye, Bye, Birdie*? The one where everyone is talking on the phone about going steady? And the kids have their own princess phones in their rooms, or they're just hanging out yapping in the den? That would never happen in my house.

"Get off that phone! The Department might be trying to call!" If it wasn't The Job, it was referred to as The Department. When I got a phone call, Mom would get out the timer and set it for five minutes. "If you can't say it in five minutes, it's not important."

My mother was great at laying on a guilt trip if I talked too long. "If your father is trying to call home and can't get through because you're on the phone, and he goes out and gets shot—I hope your conversation will have been worth it!"

If Dad called and Mom was in the bathtub, or on the toilet, I was never supposed to say that she was in the bathtub or on the toilet. I was supposed to say, "I'll get her" or "Just a minute." She'd come running to the kitchen in a towel, making wet footprints on the floor, or she'd waddle in like a duck with her pants around her knees. Mom never wanted to miss a call from Dad—she never knew whether it would be the last time they got to talk.

On Dad's days off, whenever the phone rang and Mom said, "It's The Department," it was like all the air went out of the room. Would Dad have to go in to work on a special detail? Or was it something that could wait until roll call the next day so that we could pick up where we had left off?

During the Cuban missile crisis, our phone was more than a communications device. It became a vital link in the network of the city's evacuation plan. The City of Milwaukee, with the help of the Department of Civil Defense, had devised a plan in the event of a nuclear attack. The bomb would have been dropped downtown, near City Hall. My father was to wait for the official phone call from government personnel— like an atomic bomb wouldn't knock out the phone lines? He would then proceed to Hales Corners, where the central command post would be set up. Meanwhile, we were supposed to go down in our basement and wait for the all-clear.

Every once in a while, there would be a drill. Dad would sit by the phone waiting for the call, and then he'd get in the Chevy and hightail it to Hales Corners, marking his time with a stopwatch.

The phone was also a means for people to call to ask Dad to handle their troubles. I could tell when Mrs. Kerwick was on the other end complaining about her wayward son. "Calm down, Mary. I'll get in touch with the guys in the Youth Aid Bureau, and they'll see if they can talk to him and maybe straighten him out. . . . How long has it been since you've seen him? . . . Has he called you? . . . What about his friends, have you tried talking to them? . . . Yeah, I'll talk to the sergeant. He'll come by the house. . . . Okay, Mary. Take care." Then Dad would look up phone numbers in his little brown book and call The Department and ask for Detective Sergeant So-and-So.

If the problem was really dicey, like Mrs. Plewa, Dad's cousin's wife, calling about her drunken husband, Dad would go into the basement and use the extension phone by the washing machine.

This is probably why I still don't call people up to chat. I've got a cell phone, two phone lines, call waiting, and an answering machine. But when friends calls me, I talk for five minutes. If what they have to say can't be said in five minutes—Mom was right—it's not important.

Crime Takes No Holidays

We arrived late for Christmas Eve dinner at Grandma's house. Grandma was on her knees, doing her best to dam a river of gravy. She always spilled something before a big dinner—a platter of ham, a huge bowl of mashed potatoes. She was a bottleneck in the narrow galley kitchen. In the hallway, we were bunched like commuters on a crowded bus. My glasses fogged up. My sister held onto the cheese torte. Dad carried the wine. My mother had an armful of empty cookie tins for Dad's care package.

Dad had to go to work later. We were used to it. There were home movies of Christmases past with a quick pan of the dinner table, people holding up sweaters and envelopes of cash and Dad in the background in his uniform waving good-bye before going out the kitchen door. "Crime takes no holiday," that's what he'd say.

I wished we could have gotten there earlier to get

the first pick of Grandma's Christmas cookies (I liked the pecan crescents and the spritzes, nothing with filling), but Dad was stuck in court all day.

He tried being more lenient with the populace during the days before Christmas—letting people go if they could sing all three verses of the Polish national anthem. The last thing he wanted to do was spend Christmas Eve day giving testimony and typing out reports. I'm sure he would rather have spent the day assembling that Barbie Dream House I wanted . . .

Christmas Eve was the only occasion that my cousins and I sat at the same table as the adults and ate off the good china, instead of being shoved in the back room on the crippled card table.

Grandma had been cooking for weeks. The platter piled with steaming ropes of homemade kielbasa made its way around the table. The ham went the opposite way, colliding with the mashed potatoes. The creamed corn went diagonally, followed by the rolls.

When everyone had enough food, Grandma stood at the head of the table to say grace, once in English and then, tearfully, in Polish. She used to tell us that Polish was a very romantic language. I don't know. It sounded like a record played backward to me.

Grandma went on saying a special thank you to Our Heavenly Father for keeping both her sons safe on The Job (even though Uncle Jerry worked in the office). She'd wipe away her tears with her special holiday apron. And then a toast. The adults had sparkling wine; the kids and Dad had to make do with flat Black Bear cream soda.

My mother and my aunts made obligatory comments: "The glaze on the ham, you said you used 7-Up, honey, and cloves? You must give us the recipe!" "Mother, the mashed potatoes, so creamy! Not a lump! I don't know how you do it!" Otherwise, Grandma would sulk—we'd be sorry next year because she would probably be dead, and who would do the cooking? (She had been dying every Christmas for as long as I could remember. So when I got the phone call from my father in the middle of the night twenty years later, three days before Christmas Eve, "I've got some news . . . Grandma is dead," I laughed. But it was true. It took her long enough. But she did it. We buried her in the morning and opened presents in the afternoon.)

Dad and Uncle Jerry traded stories about The Job. Dad told some of the more entertaining stuff that happened to him since they'd talked the last time. He had gotten a call about a woman who was stuck in her bathtub. The water had created suction around her. "I tried to be gentlemanly, but it was obvious that I was going to have to grab some of her fleshier parts and pull. It took two other cops and four firemen to get her out." Grandma wondered aloud whether this was proper table talk on Jesus' birthday.

Uncle Jerry related some office gossip. Just when he would get to a good part about one of the women in the office and one of the inspectors, Dad would clear his throat, signaling a change in topic.

After the dishes were scraped, washed, and put away and Grandma was satisfied with enough praise to keep her alive for another year, we'd open the presents. Dad kept a watchful eye on the clock. We had to be home by nine so that he could grab a quick nap and make roll call by 11:30 P.M.

The gifts at Grandma's were always a disappointment—usually whatever my older cousin Sue got, the rest of us got in different sizes and pastel shades. It was my only boy cousin, Marty, who got all the cool stuff. Hot Wheels, a microscope, a Ricochet Rifle (which he never got to play with—because Uncle Jerry broke it while shooting at Dad from behind the sofa).

I always hoped that the envelopes that my Grandpa handed out at the end of the gift-giving frenzy would have some significant cash value, but mine held a glitter-encrusted card with a note from Grandma: "A special Mass is being said in your honor. Boze Narodzenie, Grandma." Great. My place in Heaven was secured for another twelve months.

My grandmother's decorating scheme for Christmas was Old-World-meets plastic. She insisted on having a real tree, small enough to fit on top of a table. She hung the old ornaments (the ones that still were singed from the Great Christmas Tree Fire of 1939) and filled in any gaps with red and white plastic poinsettias and styrofoam snow balls covered in green and red sequins that she got from some mission in Guatemala for her seasonal donation. And on top of the RCA Victor color TV console (the place of honor) was the Nativity.

Grandma's Nativity scene was one of the best that I can remember. Of course, she had the key players: the wise men, the shepherds, Mary, Joseph, and the baby Jesus. She also had camels, elephants, sheiks, palm trees, dozens of sheep (with real wool), livestock, and angels. The whole set was just begging to be played with. That's why she surrounded it with Angel Hair, which according to my mother had the same potential to cut your flesh into ribbons as did the razor wire on top of the Berlin Wall. Every year my cousins and I were drawn to it, daring each other to touch it.

"Go ahead. You do it."

"No, you."

"You."

"You're the oldest."

"You're the shortest."

"You."

"No, You."

I tried it one year, attempting to move up a notch in the cousin hierarchy. I got as far as holding my hand above the silky white river of death. "Don't!" my grandmother's sister, Toots, yelled out from the kitchen. "Listen, I had a friend whose niece touched the Angel Hair, and she almost bled to death! It doesn't cut through right away; it works its way very, very slowly. When they got home, her mittens were soaked in blood." She went back into the kitchen. Okay. Well, I had gained some status. I had *almost* touched it.

The aunts helped out with the second round of food. The men retired to the basement for cards and cigars. I tried to con my way into my cousin's game of Clue. Just as the card game reached a crescendo, the aunts were telling some interesting stories about how hard it was to be well dressed during the Depression when their clothing budget was zero, and we were about to find out that it was Mr. Green in the Conservatory with the lead pipe, when Dad barked, "Get your coats!"

It was no use whining. There was no bargaining. Well, we could stay as long as we wanted and then get driven home by Uncle Louie (with the breath of death) and Aunt Toots (with the ill-fitting dentures that clicked and clacked). No, thanks. We'd go home early.

I was tucked in my bed dreaming of all the things that I was sure to get: a Barbie Dream House, a Mousetrap game, some Beatles records, a pair of big fuzzy slippers. Dad spent the night driving around the city dealing with people who had either too much holiday cheer or not enough.

On Christmas Day, it was 8:30 A.M. before Dad walked into our hallway and kicked the snow off his boots. We had been up since six, sizing up the packages under the tree, and we were ready to get to the business of present deconstruction. Santa had been good to us that year—Dad had put in a lot of overtime.

There was a battery-operated portable record player for my sister. Clothes for me. A talking Bugs Bunny hand puppet for me. A guitar for my sister that came with a warning from Dad: "No protest songs!" A new canister set and cookie jar combo for Mom. More clothes for my sister. The Mousetrap game for me. A hand warmer for Dad. A new hot seat for Dad so that his butt wouldn't get cold when he sat on a tree stump waiting to blast Bambi. And a big box in the corner with no name on it.

Dad waded through the wrapping paper to get it and handed it to Mom. She oohed and aahed over the beautiful paper and the professional wrapping job. She peeled each piece of tape off one at a time, even though Dad wanted her to just rip through the paper. She lifted off the lid, separated the tissue, and pulled out a new coat with a real fur collar. She burst into tears.

Dad fell asleep on the sofa, still in his uniform, surrounded by paper and ribbons, scotch tape stuck to the bottoms of his slippers. My sister tried to master the C chord. I figured out that Bug Bunny said only three different things. My mother made pancakes wearing her new coat over her nightgown. We woke Dad up in time for eleven o'clock mass (where he could catch a little more sleep), and then it was on to my Aunt Ellen's house to spend time with the other side of the family. Different stories. Different food. Same schedule.

Dynamic Duo

My grandmother Ceil and her sister, Toots, were born a year apart. They dressed the same. They did everything together. Maybe that was their problem.

Aunt Toots was my grandmother's older sister. The pretty one. That's what other people called her, but I remember her looking more like a bad version of a Gabor sister. As a young woman in the 1920s, Toots was all curves, not the consummate flapper—a look that came naturally to my grandmother—very skinny, no chest, like Olive Oyl. The only thing that stuck out on her were her size-twelve quad-A feet.

In Milwaukee, Wisconsin, where women with ample hips and bosoms were assured of making it through the winter and blessing their husbands with many children, my grandmother was pitied. Toots was va-va-voom.

Toots and my grandmother had an inner scale, a score sheet, and a tote board. If Grandma got herself a fur collar for her cloth coat, Toots bought herself a mink stole, complete with the head and dangling paws. If Toots was appointed secretary of the Polish Women's Alliance, Grandma had to be secretary-treasurer of her group.

It was Toots who scored first in the husband derby. She married Louie. Quite a catch. A businessman. He had his own car, smoked a pipe, and played the mandolin. Witty. Charming.

My grandmother married Martin. An okay catch. Worked in a foundry. Took the bus. Smoked cigars. Didn't own a suit. Played pinochle. Charming after several Schlitzes.

They played pinochle every Thursday night even if they weren't on speaking terms over money spent on each other's birthday gifts. Grandma channeled her card-playing strategy through my grandfather, and Toots played her hand while reading the newspaper, avoiding eye contact with her offensive sibling.

When they were speaking to each other, they went on bus tours together. To shrines with names like Our Pitiful Lady of the Sorrowful Lake. Schisms over their mother's will forgotten. So what if Toots had gotten all their mother's money! Grandma had fifteen years' worth of memories of Busia living with her, criticizing her cooking, her housekeeping, threatening to die. You can't put a dollar amount on that!

Toots was the one who got sick first. Cancer.

Grandma was diagnosed a year later. According to

her, Toots had *regular* cancer. Grandma's cancer was more rare and more involved. She had to have more doctors than Toots, more prescriptions, in-home care, and more specialists.

Toots had a priest who came to see her once a week. Grandma had her priest on call. Lists of indulgences were kept. Indulgences were numerical values assigned to prayers and good deeds. Not points, but years off a soul's stay in Purgatory. Purgatory was the place where a soul went to get purified before entering Heaven. Like a day spa with a very long line.

My grandmother kept her tally on the refrigerator next to the greasy receipts from the butcher, next to the Saint-a-Day calendar, above the thank-you letters from missionaries in Ecuador and Guatemala. Toots kept her indulgences in a little leather book on her nightstand next to the crystal rosary in the clear plastic box that had come all the way from the Vatican.

As of February 7, 1987, Toots had amassed a total of 38,535 years off for good behavior. But it wasn't good enough. Grandma was up to 42,560 years.

They died within months of each other. Toots went first, which really ticked off my grandmother. She had thought she would be the one in the express check out line: twelve sins or less. Instead, it was Toots. Well, she was the pretty one.

Easter Duty

As a kid, I dreaded Easter. In my family, Easter was not about furry bunnies and egg hunts. It was about death, torture, and loss of bodily fluids.

It started on Good Friday. My grandmother (I liked to refer to her as my Militantly Polish Grandmother) would pick me up in her big, green Buick. Every trip with her, whether it was across town or around the block, was a white-knuckle trip. Grandma never took a driver's test. She bought a car in 1929, and it came with a driver's license that she just kept getting renewed.

She was very active in all things Polish—the Polanki, the Polish Woman's Alliance—and she hoped the zeal that she had for our Polish heritage would be shared by my cousins and myself. Unfortunately, as teenagers, we thought that being Polish wasn't very glamorous. We would have preferred being Swedish. Those were the girls with the blond hair, the long legs, and the great cheekbones. We were boxy and built low to the ground, with ample hips for breeding.

Grandma was very devout. Very Catholic. She had rosaries for every occasion that she coordinated with her outfits and seasons. Pastels were for spring and summer. Black onyx with the silver cross was for funerals. The faux pearl rosary was for weddings. The crystal one, kept in its clear-plastic-covered case resting on dark blue velvet, was brought out only for something heavy duty—like when Kennedy was assassinated—it had come all the way from the Vatican.

She had a dark blue rosary for everyday use, a wooden one for Lent, a blood-red one for Good Friday, and a green and red one with a cross made up of snowflakes for Christmas. (I always thought she should have a green and gold one for Packer games, but she told me that would be blasphemous.)

On Good Friday, she took me to church for Stations of the Cross. There was a lot of genuflecting—up, down, up, down, up, down—and by the tenth station, believe me, Jesus wasn't the only one weeping. I'd try to cut corners, going halfway down, but Grandma would jab me in the ribs with her finger for every syllable:" JE-SUS-DIED-FOR-YOUR-SINS-AND-THAT'S-THE-BEST-YOU-CAN-DO?!" Or she'd point out the woman, two pews over, the one who I'm sure was wearing sackcloth underneath her shift: "She's ninety-eight, and if she can do it, so can you!"

After that, we'd hightail it across town to St.

Josaphat's Basilica for Good Friday Vigil. Three hours of silent contemplation. This is what I was contemplating: "Why am I sitting in here while all my heathen friends are running around outside?" I passed the time staring at the statues, trying to hallucinate from lack of lunch. I thought that if I stared at them long enough, maybe I would be lucky enough to see blood coming out of their eyes or see the Blessed Virgin smile at me, but no luck. I was just a bored sinner.

The next day was Holy Saturday. Grandma's Dead Tour.

My grandma had this thing about death. She attended funerals like other people go to movies or plays. Then she'd critique the clothes ("What made her want to wear that pale blue dress?"), the hair ("What was she thinking? Bangs!"), the props ("Way too much with the lilies."), the makeup ("She looked good—a lot better dead than alive!"). According to her, there were two times a woman had to look her best: when she was married and when she was buried.

We'd tour the cemetery. At each grave, Grandma would give a little background information about the occupant—cancers, heart conditions, whether the deceased still owed her money. She'd promise me that, if I was extra good, she'd treat me to something special— maybe ice cream? McDonald's? No—a trip to see her plot!

The smell of homemade kielbasa and bread filled the back seat of the car. We were taking it to get it blessed. I was tempted. Just one roll. She'd never miss it. It would have been an easy caper. Just take little bits off the bottom of the top roll. I could blame it on mice. Forget it. I didn't want to burn in hell for eternity over a lousy bun.

And then, finally, Easter Sunday. The day when all suffering was supposedly over. Easter usually falls in March or April, and in Milwaukee that usually means it's forty-five degrees and sleeting, so I had to wear my winter parka to church, over the pale yellow sleeveless dress my mother had ordered from the Penney's catalogue. At least my white shoes didn't show the salt marks.

After Mass, we'd head over to Grandma's house for some fatty, congealing ham and bad candy. Where were those rolls?

We kids were relegated to the back bedroom with a gimpy-legged card table that threatened to collapse. Normally, this would have been the primo location—it was the room with the color TV (Grandma was the first one in the family to get one), but there wasn't anything good on, just biblical epics showing the back of Jesus' head. So for entertainment we'd play this game called Pass the Spoon.

Each kid—there were six of us—had to put a piece of food on a large tablespoon. It could be anything, like ham fat or some hard thing you found in your kielbasa. (Sometimes my Grandpa stood too close to the raw meat mixture when Grandma made sausage, and some of his cigar would fall in. "Dat's for flavor," he'd say.) The one who spilled the contents of the spoon had to eat what it had held, but not before ritualistic ridicule by the lucky ones, followed by the eater's gagging and dry heaving. Nothin' like good clean kid fun!

While the aunts gossiped and washed the dishes, the uncles drove us kids to the old neighborhood. We had a ritual to perform called Kissing Busia.

Busia was my father's grandmother. She lived in the house that her husband had built for her as a wedding present in 1896. She had come from Poland to be his housekeeper, he being a widower with three small boys, but he had ended up marrying her, and together they had twelve more children.

I'm sure Busia was the sweetest thing, but she always reminded me of the witch from Disney's *Snow White*. She had sunken cheeks, missing teeth, and wispy strands of white hair escaping from her bun. She had a small hump, and she always wore black.

There she'd be. In the dark. Sitting in a chair at the end of a long, narrow hallway, beckoning us with her gnarled hands while her bachelor son, Heinie, acted as her henchman, he with the unibrow and the Wolfman hairline. He stood next to her, smiling at us, his teeth stained brown from his cigar-eating habit.

Busia smelled of Vicks, cabbage, garlic, a little brandy, and that indefinable old-person smell. We'd line up, youngest to oldest. I was always the first. My father would put his hand on the back of my coat and guide me toward her. Every year I'd pray that one of my aunts would have another kid. As I kissed her furry cheek, she'd mutter something in Polish into my ear, something that sounded like, "My, you'll cook up good in my oven!" I'd quickly turn to go, but she'd clutch me with her translucent fingers and press a Mercury-head dime into my palm. Heinie would wave me off.

On the ride home, I was always filled with a sense of relief. I was alive! Everything looked new. A great burden had been lifted. I felt renewed! Isn't that what Easter is supposed to be about?

The Home Front

My sister still thinks of herself as the Paul Revere of the Milwaukee Riots. It was July 1967. She was next door babysitting when Carl Zimmermann, the Channel Six news anchor, interrupted the *Tonight Show* to report a disturbance in the downtown Milwaukee area. All off-duty police personnel were to report to their district stations immediately.

She was the first to phone home and alert Dad. He always answered the phone after ten in case it might be a crank call, a heavy breather. He wouldn't want my mother getting all upset. He remembered how shocked she had been at the stories he had told her when he was working undercover on the Vice Squad, arresting prostitutes and men hanging around public restrooms looking for a twenty-minute relationship. She had had no idea this was going on in her city. New York, maybe Chicago, but not Milwaukee. The things people did for money!

The toilet flushing and the water running in the

bathroom sink woke me up. Then the muffled voices of my parents in the next room. The closet doors being slid open and shut. I was in bed—what was going on? Maybe somebody had died. Grandpa? Maybe one of Dad's uncles. Wouldn't surprise me if one of them were to keel over. That's what you get from chewing on LaPalina cigars for seventy years.

Maybe Dad was having one of his cluster headaches and Mom was getting ready to drive him to the hospital for a shot. I hated to see him like that—his face all red and distorted with pain. My mother leading him out of the house, Dad unable to handle looking at the streetlights. If that's what the commotion was about, I'd just as soon find out about it in the morning. But then there was the phone ringing, and Dad talking in rapid bursts of monosyllabic words and then hanging up, only to have it ring again.

Mom came into my room.

"Get up, your father is leaving for work."

"Now?!"

"Get up and say good-bye to him before he leaves. Heaven knows when we'll see him again."

Jeez. My mother could get a bit melodramatic. Like if I was having a disagreement with Dad over a family policy and the debate was still in full swing as Dad was heading out to go to work, Mom would pull me aside: "If your father goes out there and gets shot because he was distracted thinking about this silly argument . . ." She'd leave me to stew in my own guilt.

Dad was already backing the car out of the driveway.

I waved to him from the picture window. He waved back and took off.

"A riot. We're having a riot," she said in that resigned tone of voice, the one she used when she told me that we were going to have shirttail relatives stay with us for an undetermined amount of time. It was downtown somewhere. There was burning and looting and people acting crazy.

That summer there had been trouble in other big cities like Detroit and Atlanta. I watched the evening news, and people seemed so angry and frustrated. Nobody was listening to anybody. There was always a big bunch of people shouting at another bunch of people who were shouting back. Pointing fingers. Waving their fists at one another. It didn't look good.

I expected to see the glow of flames on the horizon when I looked out the front window, like the burning of Atlanta in *Gone with the Wind,* but all I saw was a raccoon coming up out of the sewer, scuttling across the street into the neighbor's yard. I went back to bed.

I got up at a more reasonable hour, when the sun was up, and went to the bathroom. Mom was on the phone in the kitchen. Shouldn't she be at work?

"Darlene, I'm not coming in today. . . . No, I'm sorry, but I'm needed at home. . . . No, I haven't heard from him. . . . He left at eleven last night. . . . Well, then, you do what you have to do, and I'll do what I have to do."

At 9:00 A.M., we were summoned into the kitchen.

My sister, still rumpled from sleeping with her head under the pillow, complained. She had fully expected to sleep until her usual 11:00 A.M. wake-up call.

Mom explained the situation. She didn't know where Dad was or when he would be coming home. As far as she was concerned, we were on high alert. Phone use was verboten. The mayor had called out the National Guard, and there was a citywide curfew from dusk to dawn. That meant we had to stay inside after supper. Mom didn't care that we lived miles from the front lines on a street that the pizza delivery guy had trouble finding. To her, dusk in July was the same as dusk in November—five o'clock. Mom leaned up against the kitchen sink and used a wooden spoon for emphasis.

During the day, we were allowed only to go up the block to our friends' houses. We had to stay within yelling range in case of an emergency. That meant we were not to hang out in our friends' bedrooms and listen to records or go into their basement rec rooms and play board games. We were supposed to hang out in their yard under the one tree, or, if it was too hot for that, we could move into their garage, but with the door open. No aimless bike riding. No walks to the library.

And another thing—she was not setting foot off the property for groceries, feminine hygiene products, or dog food until she had heard from Dad. We would have to make do. As far as everything else was concerned, the laundry, the cooking, the cleaning up, we were to carry on as usual. Understood? Dismissed. Mom's take-charge attitude was something new. Usually she was cast in a minor supporting role, and here she was Mrs. Miniver.

The phone call came two days later. Dad was okay. Yes, he was in the thick of things. That's all he could say. He'd try and call again when he could.

Mom had to settle for updates from the newspaper and the one television news station that she and my dad had bonded with—the one with the cat puppet that did the weather. There was film footage of chaos, people running, the popping of gunfire in the background, cops crouching behind squads, buildings on fire. It looked like the newsreels of the London blitz, only in color and with sound.

I kept looking for Dad. Was that him shooting a rifle from behind that row of garbage cans? Was he the one with the bloody head bending over the sewer grate? Was it him ducking into the alley between the burning buildings?

Dad surprised us the next afternoon with a stop home to change out of his tear-gassed clothing and into a fresh uniform. His newly blackened riot helmet, the white paint showing through the scrapes and dents, was on the kitchen table.

He, and a lot of other people, found out that wearing a snappy white helmet—the standard in the riot supply industry at the time—at night was like wearing a target. Cans of black lacquer spray paint were brought in by the National Guard, and all the helmets were sprayed in the underground, unventilated confines of the police garage. If someone had lit a cigarette, the whole place could have gone up.

Mom got a briefing from Dad as he changed. Things were bad. People were getting killed. The police department was ill equipped—one shotgun for every six officers. They had run out of tear gas. They were riding around in Brinks armored cars.

She worried about the basics. Was he getting enough to eat? The Red Cross was bringing in truckloads of coffee and donuts. And then, some of the shop owners offered the police sandwiches. What about sleep? He was sleeping the best he could in the brightly lit police gymnasium on a WWII army surplus cot surrounded by snoring and farting comrades.

She packed him a care package of chocolate chip cookies, the ones she baked for us (when things got tough, Mom turned to baking)—three dozen, "for the guys." Our self-imposed rationing be damned!

Mom stood on the stoop with her chin up, her nostrils flared, her hands on her hips, the wind blowing her hair. She gave him a wave. It was more like a salute than a wave. Dad sped out of the driveway in reverse and took off down the street. At least he didn't have to worry about the home front.

Dating Procedures

I was the teenage girl that everyone noticed for all the wrong reasons. I didn't have the right look for a hip teenager of the early 1970s. The hair was supposed to be blond, straight, long, and parted in the middle. My hair never fully recovered from the Toni home perms that my mother had given me while we were waiting for a new set of tubes for the TV and she was done ironing my dad's uniform shirts.

I didn't have the right clothes, either. I coveted the cool clothes and shoes that my older sister bought. She had a job working at Boston Store in the Junior department. She spent her money on taxicab-yellow plastic shoes that tied with a yellow ribbon, a lime green dress with a belt made out of metal rings, pantsuits like the ones Emma Peel wore on *The Avengers*. My mother took me shopping for my clothes at Robert Hall—a place that made J. C. Penney look trendy.

Dating Procedures

In spite of my lack of fashion sense, boys were starting to sniff around. Probably because I was the girl with the good personality. I was the girl that boys could fall back on. I became a sort of professional interim girlfriend. The one who would always be home on Friday or Saturday night as a possible Plan B. Plan C? Worst-case scenario?

To complicate matters, Dad wasn't going to allow my sister and me to date just anyone. There had to be rules. Guidelines. My father came up with a list of the types of men that we were never, ever going to be allowed to date. He called it "The Undatables." It went up on the refrigerator, right next to our daily duty roster.

Undatable number one: Men with motorcycles.

It didn't matter to Dad if they rode one—having one was just cause. Even if it had been up on cinderblocks in the garage for the past three years while they tried to get it to start, Dad was certain that one day they would get it running and take one of us for a spin around the block, and we'd end up splattered across the roadside. He had investigated too many accident scenes, scraping the scrambled-egg brain matter off the pavement. And it wasn't just a question of wearing a helmet. It was the whole motorcycle culture. To Dad, anyone with a motorcycle was a rebel without a cause. An outlaw. A no-goodnik. Someone who would never be able to hold down a decent job and be a good family man. None of them Easy Rider types in this family! I tried to point out that not all men who rode motorcycles were bad. Some were sensitive angst-filled poets like Bob Dylan. Dad rested his case.

Undatable number two: Men with tattoos.

This was not that hard to live with. The only men with tattoos that my sister and I came in contact with were the weedy, stringy-haired, greasy carnies who ran the Tilt-a-Whirl at the Wisconsin State Fair. They usually had missing front teeth and kept their cigarette packs rolled up in the sleeves of their stained shirts. Their blurry blue-green tattoos were of buxom women with "Ouch!" coming out of their mouths. Not much to disagree with there.

Undatable number three: Men with long hair.

Long hair, as my father defined it, was any hair that was longer than his. He kept his hair short. Army boot camp short. I don't think that it technically qualified as hair. It was more like a suggestion of hair. He kept it short as a matter of self-defense. His mantra was, "What's the first thing somebody grabs in a fight? Hair!"

According to Dad, "That's what's wrong with this country. There are too many kids doing whatever the hell they want, whenever they want, however they want, including growing their hair."

"But Dad, this is 1971! Besides you and the armed forces of the United States, what male over the age of six keeps his hair that short?"

Dad rested his case.

Dating Procedures

Having a cop for a father had its own panache. Boys were curious. They wanted to know what it was like to date the daughter of a cop. If it was like it was in the movies and on TV. It was sort of like dating Kitty Corleone without the paid assassins.

Dad had to be introduced to every date who crossed our threshold. The meeting took place in our small galley kitchen, right after my father got home from work so that he would still be in his uniform. His handcuffs, gun, and holster would be draped across the back of a kitchen chair, his battle-scarred nightstick resting on the counter top.

Dad would position himself right under the glare of the kitchen light, which made the creases in his face look deeper and more sinister. He fixed a sneer on his face and assumed his John Wayne stance, hands on hips, feet wide apart. This was supposed to intimidate the hell out of someone. It did.

My mother would be in the background, looking preoccupied while wiping the already clean kitchen sink. I'd be in the middle, handling the introductions.

The date would make a lame attempt at small talk, asking questions about Dad's job. Finally, his voice cracking, he would try: "Um, do you know anyone from any other municipal police departments? Because my uncle has an ex-brother-in-law who works somewhere as a deputy sheriff." Dad cocked his head to one side.

The date would continue to ramble on.

"Is your job like *Adam-12* or more like *Dragnet*?"

Nothing.

"So . . . have you ever had to shoot anyone?"

No response, except for the occasional shift in weight from one foot to the other. Then, just as the tiny beads of sweat would start to accumulate on the date's forehead, Dad would ask, "How do you spell your last name?"

My dad's brother, Jerry, was head of the Personnel Department down at HQ. He was in charge of investigating new recruits, and he would run the names of all our dates through the computer. God forbid I should go out with somebody who had a parking ticket. Dad wrote the date's name in his little brown book, then grabbed his flashlight—it was time for Vehicular Inspection.

Dad checked the headlights. The turn signals. He smelled the ashtray. Checked under the front seat. Made the date open the trunk. He made sure that there was nothing hanging from the rearview mirror. That would be a violation of state statute number 346.88 paragraph 3, subparagraph b. The one about no person shall drive any motor vehicle with any object so placed or suspended so as to obstruct the driver's clear view of the front windshield. If everything was in good working order, we were free to go.

We'd pull out of the driveway at a slow crawl, careful not to give the car too much gas. I'd make sure that my date had both hands on the steering wheel, at the ten o'clock and two o'clock positions. Then we would come to a full and complete stop at the corner of our block, even though there wasn't a stop sign. Then we would signal for the turn.

When I flipped down the visor to look in the vanity mirror, always there was Dad, still in the driveway writing down the license plate number in his little brown book, the evening sunlight glinting off his badge.

The Dance Routine

My parents sent me to an all-girl Catholic high school. My mother wanted me to go there because she remembered seeing the St. Mary's girls riding her bus in 1943, wearing their spiffy uniforms. Dad wanted me to go there to concentrate on getting a good education—not on getting a date.

St. Mary's Academy. Knowledge and Virtue United. That was the motto, carved into granite above the main entry and embroidered on the crests that were sewn onto the breast pockets of our brown wool blazers, like little badges.

We were an island of women surrounded by men—some more eligible than others. The seminarians (they were considered the lost causes) were to the south of our campus. The all-boy Catholic high school was to the west of us. On a clear day, with the wind just right, you could smell the testosterone.

Trysting wasn't impossible, but you had to be determined and stealthy. First, you had to evade the surveillance of Sister Robert. The Vatican should have sent someone to investigate her, because she had the power to be in two places at once, hear through concrete walls, and read minds.

If you made it outside, you had to pass the old nuns kneeling at the grotto meditating. They could have had anything tucked away in those voluminous sleeves. Walkie-talkies? Cameras? Binoculars?

Past the grotto, you had to cut through the swamp and navigate the woods, being careful not to make a wrong turn because that would put you smack dab in the middle of the nuns' graveyard. Nothing put the kibosh on a lust-filled rendezvous faster than the eyes of Saint Francis of Assisi watching your every move. The nuns patrolled the grounds, and Dad patrolled everything else. He could be anywhere at anytime. It was like living with a supreme being.

He was assigned to the Police Department's tactical unit, or the Tac Squad, as they called it. It was supposedly a stealthy, quasi undercover unit that handled everything from hostage situations to the potentially troublesome large-group gathering. The entire city was his beat. He rode around in an unmarked squad, but come on: four middle-aged white guys in matching navy blue windbreakers and crew cuts driving around in dented brown Plymouths with the little chrome hub caps didn't need the words "Milwaukee Police Department" on the doors.

Dad could spot a wise guy across a crowded room and anticipate trouble before it started. This was why the nuns at my school always asked him to chaperone our dances. I remember one dance in particular—the one that Dad didn't chaperone. He had to work.

I had spent the better part of two weeks before the dance checking with my informants to find out whether the boy, the one with the wavy copper-colored hair, wire-rimmed glasses, and army jacket, the one who got on my bus two stops after me, was going to be there. He was.

Our dances were held in the gym under the jurisdiction of Coach Louise Burdick. She was addressed simply as "Coach." Never Coach Louise or Miss Burdick. It was hard to tell whether she was a miss or a mister.

She wore slacks (without a fly). No evidence of a penis that I could see, but, then again, GI Joe didn't have one either. A short-sleeved shirt, no evidence of breasts whatsoever, with the top button open at the neck, revealing her white cotton undershirt. She had two pairs of shoes—Black Chuck Taylor canvas high-tops for everyday and black referee shoes for special occasions. Her only piece of jewelry was a shiny, chrome whistle on a leather lanyard. Her hair was cut in a low-maintenance, no-nonsense style.

The Dance Routine

Coach was very territorial about the gym floor. She kept it polished to a high gloss. During the dances she roamed the periphery, making sure that no one was necking in the corners or, worse, leaving scuffmarks.

There were so many kids crowded into our gym from the area Catholic high schools that the walls would get wet with condensation. We really didn't do a lot of dancing per se. We had live bands. The music was full of twenty-minute-long guitar solos. Most of the kids just stood around, nodding their heads to the riffs.

I observed the copper-headed boy's modus operandi. I knew which wall he leaned up against, when he went for soda, and when he went to the bathroom. The moment he was separated from the rest of his friends, I went over to talk to him. "Stairway to Heaven." That's the song the band was playing. A song that we couldn't dance to, so all we did was sort of hang on each other and sway. It was heaven.

Just when the boy was about to make his move, the band stopped playing. Coach was on the bandstand next to the be-fringed, big-haired lead singer, telling everyone to leave the gym in an orderly fashion. There was a bomb scare.

No time to grab my coat. The boy gallantly offered me his. Hmmmmm. It had a nice smell of army surplus and Brut. We were herded across the street. It was February. Clouds of our breath filled the night air. I shivered under the armpit of my newfound love. Sirens screamed in from all directions. It felt like one of those movies about World War II, where the two doomed lovers are trapped in a crowded train station, trying to get out of the city before the Nazis march in. It was all so romantic.

Until that dented brown Plymouth pulled up.

Sketchy Details

It was 1973. I was enrolled as a liberal arts student at the University of Wisconsin–Milwaukee. Dad and I had decided that the liberal arts were the way to go, until I figured out what I wanted to major in. Dad hoped I would pick a career like nursing or teaching. Or my mother's dream job—a librarian.

He gave me all kinds of advice as I tried to pick the right classes from the thick course description book. His opinions had been formed by years of driving around in squads complaining with his partners about the kids today and how they weren't amounting to anything: a girl should go to college, get a degree, get a good job, or at least find a husband with the potential for getting a good job. Even if I never used my degree, at least I'd have a backup.

Dad had a linear view of college. You sit down one evening, decide what you want to be, take the classes, and get good grades, and, at the end of four years, you have a piece of paper that gets you a good-paying job; voilà, you're set for life.

UWM was not my first choice of schools. I wanted to go to Madison, where the bulk of my friends were going, but my older sister put the kibosh on that plan. She had planned to go to the University of Wisconsin–Stevens Point. Toured the campus with Mother. Registered. Enrolled. Had a dorm room. Dad had grudgingly filled out all the necessary financial forms. She lasted three days. She called home in tears because she missed her big galoot of a boyfriend, her reason for living, the reason my father wanted her miles away and surrounded by potential replacements.

Dad tried to talk some sense into her, practicing the negotiation skills he had picked up in a hostage situation training seminar, but it didn't work. After that fiasco, and the loss of a semester's worth of tuition and room and board, he issued an official memorandum: From that day forward, he would not be paying for anyone's college tuition. He would pay for books and supplies, that's it.

I took botany not because I had a lofty goal of finding the cure for cancer but because I thought it would make me a better forest ranger. Which is what I thought I wanted to be in life, and it was the only class I could think of.

Dad was thrilled. He thought all those camping trips to Glacier National Park in Montana and the Black Hills of South Dakota had finally paid off. To him, being a forest ranger was a good career. A job in the great outdoors. And a uniform and a badge were involved.

We sat at the kitchen table, filling out my intended schedule with classes in botany, English, sociology, and anthropology. I had room for one more class, and the voice of my high school art teacher, Sister Sylvia, reverberated in my head, telling me how talented I was. How I should really consider majoring in art. But in high school it was more like crafts than art. I registered for Drawing 101.

Finding my classes the first day of college was nothing like it had been in high school. There was a map involved. Instead of negotiating hallways crowded with girls in plaid skirts, I had to traverse city blocks, avoiding speeding mopeds.

When I finally found the botany lab, I knew I was already in trouble. The course description listed high school biology as the only prerequisite, which was a big lie. It should have also listed the required personality type and the thought processes involved.

The other students had already assigned themselves lab partners, the same ones they had had in their senior year at high school, and were working on the first experiment in the lab manual. I was the odd person out. I had to work alone.

They made up jokes with the words "pistil" and "stamen" in the punch lines. They had spent the summer conducting experiments for extra credit. The only thing I had worked on over the summer was saving the unsuspecting public from the insidious spread of foot fungus at a county pool and getting a good tan.

Our first lab assignment was to discuss how and why plants wilt and to conduct an experiment to support our findings. This was due in two weeks. Simple enough. Two plants. One container of water. Wait and see.

I observed the specimens. I illustrated my findings. I was so proud. I filled two entire pages in the manual! I was certain that I had done a great job, until I got to class. Some reports were half an inch thick, bound in simulated black leather. The titles took up four or five lines. I had two beautifully drawn illustrations, influenced by the scientific drawings of Audubon, one of a wilted plant with the words "needs water" underneath and the other of a lush, vibrant plant with the words "doesn't need water" next to it. At least I could see the progress I'd made in my drawing class.

When I got the manual back from the teaching assistant, he wrote next to the big red F in the corner, "See me after class." He asked me what my goals were. I told him about my idea of becoming a forest ranger. He asked me why. Was I passionate about the outdoors? Well, I liked camping. But what was it that really interested me? It was obvious to him that I had a talent for drawing. And, yes, that did interest me, but what was I supposed to do with it? What would a degree in art get me besides a worried father?

When I walked into the drawing studio filled with tatami mats, the soft tinkling of chimes coming from somewhere, the smell of patchouli wafting down the hallway, I felt at ease. The kids were in various positions, propped against tie-dyed pillows or slouched on the wooden drawing benches. A few makeshift turbans stuck out from behind the huge pads of drawing paper. The professor arranging today's still life—deer antlers, a rusty bucket, some paisley fabric, shoes, an old toaster—was making comments about how we need to focus on the negative space. What we don't draw is as important as what we do draw. I understood everything he said.

To Dad, a job was something you did to pay the bills. It wasn't something you were born to do. Dad wanted to become a teacher, but he couldn't afford to go to college, so his Plan B was to be a cop. That's how he would get to work with kids. He wanted to help the juvenile delinquents get turned around before they did something that got them into serious trouble. The work also paid the bills.

Dad came home from work in a good mood. It was a quiet day in the city. No major altercations. People had behaved themselves. The planets must have been in some strange alignment.

"I've decided that I'm going to major in art."

"Major in art? Are you nuts!? I thought you were going to be a forest ranger? What happened to that?" I showed Dad the lab manual with the big red F in the corner. I told him about Sister Sylvia, what the teaching assistant had said, and my feelings about my drawing class and how it was all pointing me in the right direction. I told him that I had found My People.

My people, according to Dad, were freaks. Weirdos. The same ones he had to deal with at the Alternate Site, a piece of the park across the street from Lake Michigan where there were free concerts until 10:00 P.M. These were the kids who threw bags of feces at him and called him a pig when he was only trying to do his job. They were all pot-smoking, anti-American subversives who didn't care about the laws of this country. He was worried that I was going to end up in Haight-Ashbury or, at the very least, on Brady Street.

"What about Ralph?" I asked. My father's cousin was an artist. A painter.

Ralph was the oddball. He wore red polka-dotted socks and huarache sandals while the other guys wore brown socks and brown Hush Puppies. He had a beat-daddy goatee. He drove a little blue foreign car. Dad described Ralph's paintings as "A bunch of boxes and lines with some big red blobs in the middle."

I thought Ralph was fun. He used to draw caricatures at our family picnics. All the kids would hang around him, including me. We would watch him start out with a blank piece of paper and, with a few lines, capture Uncle Heinie perfectly: his unibrow, that Wolf-man hairline, the little brown teeth, the cigar in the corner of his mouth. It was magic.

"Maybe it's genetic," offered my mother.

"I could always get a job teaching, like Ralph." I had no intention of being a teacher, but I thought it would make Dad happy. The fact that Ralph was gainfully employed by the Milwaukee Public School System nine months out of the year legitimized him in Dad's book.

I showed him some of the drawings in my sketchbook and pointed out the professor's comments about my astute use of line, my ability to capture the essence of the object. Dad quickly looked them over.

"Maybe you could get a job as a police sketch artist," he said. I'd seen those drawings in the newspaper. It looked like someone just picked a face shape (oval, square, round) and added the features from a collection of eyes, lips, and noses. It was like the Police Department's version of Mr. Potato Head.

This was a breakthrough. Dad was warming up to the idea.

Rangemaster

Dad's respected role model, Harold Breier, retired from the force. A new chief of police took the helm, and he wanted things run efficiently and in an up-to-date way. He wanted top people for critical positions in The Department. Especially at the Academy. That's where it all started. With the new recruits. Got to train 'em right from the get-go. He needed somebody who had experience. Who was organized. Who liked dealing with young cops and showing them the ropes.

The Chief could have brought in somebody from across the country, but why look for someone in Kansas City or Montana when he had just the guy for the job of Rangemaster right here? Dad.

But Dad wasn't too thrilled. To him, the job involved a desk, which made it a desk job—and when a guy in The Department was taken off the street and given a desk job, that meant he was either under investigation or they were trying to tell him that he couldn't cut it anymore.

A desk job? Regular hours? Weekends and holidays off? Mom thought it was a dream come true. After twenty-eight years, she was finally going to get some sleep at night.

Dad remembered the oath he had taken back in 1950 to serve, to protect, and to obey his superior officers. Even if they wanted him out of a squad and in front of a classroom. He reported for duty at the Police Academy.

Dad was in an unfamiliar landscape. His desk contained a phone, an in/out basket, and a blotter from some ammo supplier. No clutter. No fluff. He had a few photos of his loved ones on the wall (his springer spaniels, Belle and Duke) and a picture of the guys, smiling in a soggy duck blind. His framed firearms certification hung on the wall next to the certification from the FBI Academy.

There were meetings to attend, lesson plans to type, phones to answer, and different kinds of paperwork to fill out. He had to take sensitivity training—to get in touch with his inner cop.

There was no one left at home for him to pass on life lessons to. I was married and had two small children. My sister lived close enough to pop in for dinners but far enough away to keep her sanity. My mother could take only so much of Dad's pontificating before she would go out shopping. Then he'd be home alone, with his dogs, watching *Barney Miller* reruns. When he stood in front of his first class of forty recruits, their eyes wide open, their ears perked up, eager to hear what he had to say, he figured that maybe this was going to be all right.

These kids laughed at all his corny jokes. They did exactly what he told them to do, how and when he said to do it. There was no whining. No "Mom said that it was okay for me to do it this way." No "Yeah, I'll get to it when the next commercial comes on." Nobody sassed him. Nobody questioned his authority. It was his way or the highway.

The day that the recruits received their weapons, Dad couldn't just go around the room and pass out the guns like Sister Gregory had done with the extra pencils: "Take one and pass the rest back to your neighbor." No, there had to be more drama to it. After all, this piece of equipment was meant to save their lives and the lives of others. He had a John Wayne approach to giving a lecture.

"Awright. Listen up!" he growled. Each desk had a bright yellow box on it. Dad told the recruits not to touch the boxes. Not even to look at them until he told them to. Dad explained the various parts of the weapon, the proper way to handle it, how to load it, and how to clean it. He paused for effect. Then, when the only sound was the ka-chunk of the minute hand of the clock on the wall, he said, "Take your gun out of the box and put it in your grubby paws." It was like Christmas morning.

Dad didn't have any problems with the female recruits in the class. He treated them the same way he treated me—like a man. He expected them to play with the little hurts, to walk them off. There was no room in his class for broken nails, for PMS, for crying. "Cut that out!" he'd bark. "What the hell are you gonna do out on the street? Blubber like a baby?" Dad would add something to break the tension: "You'd never see John Wayne cry. Not even in *The Sands of Iwo Jima*. Although, when he got shot at the end, I admit, I got a little misty."

There was only one instance when he had to treat the women differently—when it came time to order ballistic vests. They had to be made to measure, to accommodate a woman's figure. He thought that the women would be able to fit into smaller men's sizes, as I had when I was growing up. He bought me boy's hiking shoes and boy's jeans and T-shirts until I couldn't fit into them; then the outfitting duty was passed on to my mother.

Only this time, there was no mother to pass on the duties to. Dad had to order the vests, which were made like corsets. Just think of them as armor, he reminded himself, and he was okay with that.

The recruits were all weaned on TV cop shows: *Hill Street Blues, Streets of San Francisco, Hawaii Five-O, Kojak*. To Dad, these shows were unbelievable. Total fiction. "The day I'd walk into the Captain's office and tell him that he was full of it, you think I'd have a job the next day?" Cop shows had too many officers doing things that were against regulations. Shooting their guns in every episode (not taking careful aim), wasting city resources ("If I smashed up as many cars as they do, I'd be written up so many times I'd be filing papers until retirement").

At the outdoor range, there was always one kid who would try to do one of those drop-roll-and-shoot moves like all the TV cops did, only he would miscalculate his rotation and end up pointing the wrong end of the loaded weapon at the wrong target—Dad—who would have a few choice words to say.

Action. Excitement. Adventure. This is what these kids expected. Dad tried to give them reality checks. He told them that the job was tedium and paperwork, paperwork, paperwork. He said that in his thirty years on The Job, he had fired his gun maybe three times.

They'd ask about his experiences. He'd tell them about the bodies he had pulled out of the Milwaukee River (green floaters), about fighting with guys crazy with drink, about rolling down the street, about trading punches, and about finding drunks folded in half and stuffed into empty barrels, perfectly fine, not remembering how they had gotten there. He told them about being the first to arrive at an accident scene and trying to find the victim's other arm, which made it sound a lot like a TV show and didn't help his case. He taught them practical stuff, like how to deal with a dead body that had been in an apartment for a few days: "Smoke a cigar before you go in. It helps tone down the stink and settle your stomach." And when to shoot their weapon: "Never take your gun out of the holster unless you mean to use it. All those cops on television and in the movies who have the gun out and are threatening to shoot if the criminal doesn't drop the knife, gun, bat, that's not the way it works."

He had a driving course set up on the parking lot in the back of the Academy. He made the recruits drive it rain or shine, ice or snow. Dad would ride along in the car, barking out orders: "Turn left! Turn right! No! I mean, turn left!" The recruit at the wheel would take the necessary actions, sometimes sliding into the huge piles of snow left by the plow or spinning out on the patches of ice in front of the retired nuns from the Sisters of Mercy. They lived in one of the other buildings on the grounds. When the recruits were on the driving range, the nuns would sit outside on their lawn chairs all bundled up, applauding. A far cry from Dad's teaching me how to drive in the parking lot of Sentry or Forest Home Cemetery.

Sometimes, I'd run into cops working at Summerfest or sitting in a squad somewhere, and I'd ask them if they knew my dad, the Rangemaster. An immediate bond formed.

"He's your Dad?

"Yeah."

"Tell me, did he tell all those corny jokes?"

"Yeah."

"Did he make you do stuff over and over and over until you got it done his way?"

"Yeah."

"You know, he was tough. And now that I've been out on the street for five years, he was right about everything."

"Yeah, I know."

Ponytail Girl Et Al.

Dad taught me well. If ever I spotted anyone suspicious, I was supposed to get a good look at the person, remember the person's clothing, height, and weight, and, if the person was in one of those big sedans, get the license number.

Whenever we drove around, he'd quiz me. "What kind of car is behind us? Quick! What was the license plate number of that car that just turned left! How many people were standing at the bus stop? Who had on the camel overcoat?"

I practiced memorizing license plate numbers, noting what people wore, whether they had any moles or scars. You never know when skills like this could come in handy.

Tuesday, June 12.

Ponytail Girl was back. She was dressed for the humid weather in a breezy sarong with a tiny white tank top and strappy flat sandals. Her long, brown hair was tied up in her trademark style. I saw her ring the doorbell of the bungalow across the street, turn to look up and down the block, and adjust her skirt before a guy in a not-so-stylish tank top and shorts opened the aluminum storm door to let her in.

When my husband came home from work, the temperature was still in the high eighties. We decided to cook out.

"Something is going on across the street," I said to him, as he slapped the raw chicken on the crusty grill.

"Really? How do you know? Do you do like a Gladys Kravitz kind of thing and peek out of the drapes all day?"

"Noooo! I look up from whatever I'm doing and I just see things," I snapped back. I never peeked. That was for amateurs. In extreme cases, I used binoculars.

"You *see* things." He said it in a tone that implied I was having visions.

"Yes."

"Like what kinds of things?" Flames shot up around the chicken. He doused them with his beer.

"Well, like today . . . Ponytail Girl rang the door bell of the house across the street, and the guy came and let her in."

"Ooooo, very suspicious!"

I was used to getting mocked by him and by the police. I admit, the first time I called the police, I wasn't sure how to say exactly what it was that I saw.

"Milwaukee Police—" The officer who answered the phone mumbled his name. He sounded like he already knew that my complaint was hardly worth the effort it took him to pick up the phone after fourteen rings.

"Um, yeah. Hi. Um, I'd like to report some kind of suspicious behavior?" See, that was my first mistake, ending my statement like it was a question. It gave the officer an easy target.

"What?! Is it suspicious or what?!"

"Um, oh yeah! There's this house—"

"What about it?"

"Well, people come and go—"

"Lady, people come and go all the time."

"Right, right. I know, but—"

"Are there any weapons? Do you see any guns?"

"No. No weapons. But, see, there's this girl, well, there's been a couple of girls. Different ones from time to time that I've noticed and they come up to the door and knock or sometimes they ring the bell—"

"Uh huh. They ring the bell, and?"

"And the guy comes and lets them in! But—"

"What guy?"

"The guy who lives there."

"And this is suspicious to you?"

I just hung up. Embarrassed. Maybe I was turning into a Gladys Kravitz! No one believed her when she witnessed Endora changing Darren into a pig. She'd call her husband, Abner, over to the window, but he'd get there too late. Samantha would have Darren changed back to good ol' Darren right before Larry Tate got there and Abner would gently lead Gladys away from the window to get her the pills.

But, there *was* something going on across the street. Not every day. Sometimes weeks, months would go by, and everything would be normal. The guy would come out and cut his grass. He'd chat with the mailman. I don't know, it wasn't right.

Kids started hanging around. During school hours. Kids with cell phones. They wore pants with the left leg pulled up and baseball hats tipped to the right. Occasionally a tricked-out car with black windows would come by and make a pit stop. The guy would come out, take something from the car, and scamper back into the house.

Pretty soon it wasn't just Ponytail Girl who would come and go. There was Monica (I named her after Monica Lewinsky because of the kicky beret she wore), Kate Moss (she was runway-model thin and had long, straight hair), and Ally McBeal.

I first noticed Ally McBeal standing on the corner near the bus stop. She was dressed in a nice business-woman's suit with matching pumps and a Kate Spade–type of a handbag. She stood out from the usual crowd of unattractive people who waited for the bus in their oversized T-shirts, sweatpants, and Packer jackets.

"Look! And you're always complaining about the women in our neighborhood," my husband said.

"Yeah, I know."

"What did you say the other day? How you never see any, like, professional women—"

"Other than hookers," I interjected.

"Yeah, other than hookers, at the bus stop? Now, look. There was a perfect example. See? I'm always telling you that there are a lot of white-collar, managerial-type people who live in our neighborhood! You just don't notice them. You're too obsessed with the bad elements. She's obviously going to work. She must work downtown somewhere. That's an expensive suit. She's well put together—" I had to interrupt his pontificating.

"Too bad she has an Adam's apple," I said.

For two years I kept tabs on that house. My police communications skills improved. I learned to cut to the chase. I learned not to deal with the regular Joe who answered the phone at the district station. I had the Vice Squad on speed dial.

"Vice. Detective Piontek."

"I'd like to report some prostitution." I rattled off descriptions, the address of the house, the circumstances, whom I saw doing what to whom, where and when. The detective took notes. Asked pertinent questions. Made me repeat things so that he could get it right. "Hey, hand me that file . . . on that cabinet over there . . . yeah, that one. . . . Um, hey, are you going to be home tonight, like, say around eight or nine?"

"Are you talking to me?" I said.

"Yeah, are you gonna be home? 'Cause I think me and my crew is going to be paying those people a visit. So's you may want to, like, grab a bowl of popcorn and get a good seat. It's gonna be good."

At ten to eight I casually took a look out the front window. To, um, see whether I had turned off the sprinkler. Ponytail Girl sat on the front stoop, portable phone in hand. She motioned to a car with a neon undercarriage and tinted windows to pull over. If ever there was a perfect setup, this was it. I had had my hopes dashed before. The squad would pull up ten minutes too late, the perps long gone. "Come away from the window, Gladys, and I'll get you your pills."

Boom! Tires squealed. Unmarked and marked squads blocked the street. A big, burly guy with a leather vest and a blond mullet chased Ponytail Girl and tackled her as she ran toward the alley. The guy bolted out of the driver's side door of his slick midnight-blue low rider; fortunately, the car wasn't the only thing that was low riding—he tripped over his saggy, baggy shorts and was promptly sat on by two beefy vice squad officers. Two other cops in bulletproof vests busted down the front door of the bungalow. Guns were drawn. Two guys were led out to the waiting van in cuffs. It was like a scene from *Cops*.

Two days later, I got the phone call I'd been waiting for.

"Hey, this is Detective Piontek. Did you happen to catch the action the other night?"

"I did! It was a thing of beauty."

"Well, I gotta tell you, we got the hooker, her pimp, her dealer, and when we got them downtown, they gave us more names. Yeah, this turned out to be a nice bust. And if it wasn't for you, we woulda never known this was going on."

Crime fighting. It's in my blood.

Cop Switch-Off

When Dad retired from The Job, he had been a cop for almost forty years. I wasn't too worried about how he would adjust to his life without crime, mayhem, and paperwork. He told me that when he turned in his badge, he turned off the cop switch.

There were other guys who had left The Job before him.

They sat around the house for the first three weeks trying to think of a hobby to get into. Woodcarving? Home brewing? Then they'd spend countless hours at the library doing research and ordering equipment before they figured out this hobby wasn't for them and all the stuff went into the to-be-rummaged pile in the garage.

There were other guys who just followed their wives around the house all day criticizing the way they did the dishes, where they did the shopping, and how they folded the sheets. They'd sit in the La-Z-Boy recliner and watch the street in front of the house, wondering what that kid was up to, the one standing by that car over there, thinking, "If I were still on The Job, I'd go out and do a field interview." But now they were just some old geezer in the neighborhood who mowed his lawn in teal shorts.

But Dad had his dogs.

He bought his first purebred dog when I was eighteen. He had replaced our late, paunchy fourteen-year-old Humane Society black Lab mix with a solid rocket of a springer spaniel. My mother was shocked at the sticker price.

He joined a kennel club and had a new circle of friends who were not involved in law enforcement. Every chance he got, he'd be out at the kennel club running his dog. Rain or shine. Winter. Summer.

One short peep of the whistle, and she would come to a screeching halt and sit down. Two short peeps of the whistle, and she'd stop whatever she was doing and come running back to him and sit at his feet. One long peeeeeeep and a short pip, and she'd be off and running. I always thought it more than a coincidence that he got into training this dog when I started college and was totally untrainable (when he blew the whistle at me, I wouldn't heel or sit).

There were offers for him to work. How'd he like to be a security guard nights at some factory? He'd be able to carry a loaded weapon. Patrol the grounds in a car. Watch out for anybody trying to vandalize the property.

"No, thanks." That interfered with the upcoming field trial in Michigan.

Would he care to be a bodyguard for some multi-millionaire who had homes in Sarasota, Florida, and in Palm Springs and spent summers at his small estate in River Hills? Free travel! He'd need someone to stay at the estate while he was in Europe. "Nope, sorry, too busy." Dad had to shoot at the kennel club's hunting test, and he was on the kennel club's board of directors in charge of planning the year's events.

Calls came from technical schools that had courses in police science. Would he mind being a guest lecturer for their firearms course? "Nope." He had to check out a litter of springers in East Troy.

Dad had fishing and hunting trips with the guys to Canada and Wyoming to plan. He didn't have to worry about trying to cajole somebody into switching days off with him. He went to the Milwaukee *Journal-Sentinel* sport show during the day, collected his weight in all kinds of brochures, and didn't have to fight the crowds.

There was a fight in front of my parents' house—kids in the street, cars squealing around the turn, enough shouting to wake my mother up. She went to the window to see what was happening. She ran back to the bedroom and nudged Dad, who was snoring blissfully.

"Wake up! There's a fight or some kind of rumble thing going on down at the corner!"

"Call the district station and tell them about it." He readjusted his pillow and turned over. He had done his tour of duty. Let one of those gung-ho kids fresh out of the academy take the call. He had an early morning with the dogs.

The relatives still called up any time one of my cousins got into trouble. Dad held the cordless phone with one hand and flipped through the pages of his latest issue of *Gun Dog* with the other, while my aunt explained the situation.

Every couple of pages, Dad uttered an obligatory "Uh huh," and then, when he got to the ads in the back of the magazine, he offered his advice: "Pay the fine, or visit him in jail." End of magazine. End of conversation.

Being a cop by convenience didn't always work. Driving with the guys to Canada for their fishing jamboree, Dad got pulled over by a Minnesota state trooper for speeding. He was just trying to pass this truck. And he had to punch it up to eighty to get back into the lane.

"What's that?" asked the trooper, eyeing the miniature version of his old badge that Dad kept pinned in his wallet next to his driver's license.

"Oh, we're all retired Milwaukee police officers."

"Then you should know better. Two points and $135."

Five years after Dad retired, if there was some police action going on in my neighborhood, I'd walk up to the cop sitting in the squad, work my father's name into my introduction, and get the lowdown on any arrests being made or perpetrators who might be still at large. The cop always asked about Dad: "Hey, how's the Rangemaster doing? Keeping busy?"

Seven years, eight years, ten years went by, and I'd mention his name to the cops standing at the Port-A-Johns at the Circus Parade. They didn't recognize it. I gave them the background on him. That he worked on the Vice Squad, the Youth Aide Bureau, the Ambulance Detail, and the Tactical Unit. That he was in the Riots of '67, that he received a Class D citation for bravery for talking a guy out of shooting his girlfriend. That he started out walking a beat downtown and ended up being in charge of firearms training at the academy.

He had seen it all. And he and I both lived to tell about it.